Mark Price was born in the midst of the 1950s wool boom and regularly, through those golden years, caught the bus from the family farm in West Otago to the 52-strong Wikoikoi Primary School. In between times, he chased sheep, made hay, caught eels, shot rabbits and fought with his siblings. Employment followed high school, first as a cadet reporter, then mostly working in the daily news media, including TV1, TV3 and of late, the *Otago Daily Times*.

Mark lives in Dunedin with La Campaña and the expedition members, and has already completed a second trip to Spain, with La Campaña, this time by bicycle.

He is the author of *Getting Away with Murder: The Jennifer Beard Inquiry.*

ANTIPODES

The Ingenious and
Exhilarating Expedition
of El Líder and
La Campaña

Mark Price

Longacre Press

Acknowledgements

My thanks to Bill McLean who read Jerome K. Jerome's *Three Men in a Boat* to his classroom of country kids and had them laughing 'til they cried. Thanks to my parents for steering me away from farming and forestry and into journalism.

Thanks to Barbara Larson at Longacre Press for her bravery.

Thanks to Brian Grant at the School of Surveying, University of Otago, for generously giving his time and expertise.

Thanks to those who worked on the book — Penelope Todd and Christine Buess at Longacre; Andrew Frampton at Colortronics; James Barnsley and Wayne Chettleburgh.

Thanks, of course, to the members of the expedition and, above all, thanks to Cathy who makes every day an adventure.

ISBN 978 1 877460 36 4

A catalogue record for this book is available from the National Library of New Zealand.

First published by Longacre Press, 2009
30 Moray Place, Dunedin, New Zealand.

Book and cover design by Christine Buess
Photography by Mark Price
Colour imagery by James Barnsley
Maps by Brian Grant and Andrew Frampton
Printed by Everbest Printing Company Ltd in China

www.longacre.co.nz

INTRODUCTION

When he was young, he travelled much. And when finally he returned to New Zealand, he had many tales to share. If anyone asked. Which no one ever did.

In contrast to Stanley's search for Livingstone, Scott's quest for the Pole, and Hillary's Everest climb, HIS overland trip to Clacton-On-Sea, HIS bus journey through Belgium, and HIS scaling of the Alps by funicular railway, had gone entirely unnoticed.

What had seemed at the time to be daring adventures were, he now conceded, mere tourist trips. Holidays.

And as time went by, they faded from his memory to the point where they might never have happened.

Since his travelling days, he had passed the years quietly, doing family-raising things in a tidy, two-storey plaster home in a suburb of Dunedin.

He rarely ventured far. Journeys in his youth had been spontaneous and random; now they consisted of dreary, daily drives to a dingy office.

If he went further afield, it was only to familiar places. He had negotiated the same roads, the same traffic hazards, the same views, the same lunch-stops, for more than twenty years.

And at the end of each office-job-day, his habit was to recline, exhausted, on an Italian-leather couch and watch the world pass by on his television set while his wife prepared tea.

It was a comfortable life.

One cool Dunedin evening, as he sipped his one, small, after-work bottle of beer in the warm glow from the wood fire in the corner of the lounge, and as the sound of clattering from the kitchen obscured the sound of the television news, he was visited by an idea.

It wafted into his mind, vague and shapeless, and threatened to waft straight on out again.

He sat up suddenly, turned away from the television set and stared hard at nothing in particular.

And there it was. The idea.

He would create an expedition.

He would find something that was unexplored and set about exploring it.

He lay back on the couch and noticed that he had missed the sports news.

Evening after evening he returned to the idea. The trick, he reasoned, would be to find something requiring the vision and single-mindedness of the great explorers, but without, perhaps, so many of the hardships. Like the cold.

In fact, he decided that he would only set out on an expedition that could be conducted in temperatures above 15 degrees Celsius. That was the first rule. He was tempted to add others that would prohibit eating sled-dogs and drinking his own urine, but he did not want to seem frivolous.

So he imposed no other limit on the scope of possible expeditions, though he felt there were some things he would prefer not to do — such as channel swimming, or long-distance running, or cycling or anything to do with heights, horses or going underground. Or rowing.

Unfortunately, many of the best ideas had long since been taken: discovering the source of the Nile and that sort of thing.

He had recently read of a man and his son who had kayaked from the middle of Canada to the middle of South America, so that had been done.

There were the two Englishmen who had bicycled to the point on the earth — in Mongolia — farthest from the sea, and there was the first woman to sail solo around the world against the prevailing winds.

It took months of daydreaming but eventually it came to him — an expedition idea that was suitably unique and challenging. Perfect. Perfect because it was simple. It was an idea as simple as climbing the highest mountain in the world or crossing the Gobi Desert on a camel.

HE would explore the antipodes of New Zealand.

It occurred to him that New Zealand's antipodes might never have been explored before and that, chances were, he would be exploring a place that was pristine. There would be none of Sir Ed's footprints to follow. There would be no empty oxygen bottles, shredded tents, tin cans, plastic bags or skeletons to trip over. In expedition terms, this would be virgin territory.

In a fit of excitement, he rolled off the couch, ran downstairs, rummaged in a cupboard, and found a globe his son had once been given for a birthday. He blew it up and put one finger on Wellington and one on the other side of the globe, and twirled it. New Zealand's antipodes seemed to be somewhere in Spain. How many people knew that?

'Not very many,' he felt like shouting.

Over the next few days he rolled the idea around in his mind. It developed. Matured. An expedition name came to him. This would be 'A Journey to the Ends of the Earth'.

And knowing now that the other end of the earth was in Spain, he felt the need to create a title for himself that would acknowledge the Spanish connection. He decided he should be 'El Líder de la Expedición'.

As for his good wife, he knew it would be unwise to suggest a title with a lesser status so decided that, if she wished, she could be 'Encargado de la Campaña'—or campaign manager.

PART

1

THE
NEW ZEALAND END
OF THE EARTH

The New Zealand End of the Earth

1

PREPARATIONS

El Líder—as he was beginning to refer to himself—
considered for a long moment where an explorer might
begin 'A Journey to the Ends of the Earth'.

As a child, he had been told that if he was to dig a hole
straight down he would get to China. Clearly, someone had made
a mistake.

El Líder reached for his computer, brought up the Google
homepage and typed in 'antipodes', 'antipodean', 'ends of the earth',
'four corners of the earth', 'the other side', 'earth circumference'
and 'earth diameter'.

In a weekend he used up a whole month's worth of Xtra
downloading time. He found sites with 'antipodes' in their titles
that sold clothing and bottles of water, and others specialising in
poetry and parakeets.

He found a crude map of the earth with—superimposed over
the top—an upside-down mirror version of the same map. It
showed how rare it was for land masses to have antipodes on other
land masses.

North America, for instance, fell in the Indian Ocean, so to
get to the antipodes of New York would require a ship. And the
same could be said of all the great cities of the world—London,
Sydney, Paris, Rome, Moscow and Dubai. It brought home to
El Líder the rarity of the relationship between New Zealand and
Spain.

No website that he could find delved into this relationship, and that confirmed, to El Líder's delight, that a knowledge-hole existed and that it would take an expedition to fill it.

Over the course of six months, his thoughts rarely strayed from 'the other side'. Certainly, the hall stairway did get painted, he tended the office job, he kept track of Coronation Street and he mowed the lawn regularly. But these were distractions from the real business of expedition planning.

El Líder thought of Burke and Wills, Speke, Mungo Park and that other chap who discovered China. Although he believed his expedition idea was as fine as theirs, it lost a little of its focus in the area of what exactly it might achieve.

He knew he would not return home with exotic plants and animals or chests of gold or maps of never-before-seen lands. And it would just not be enough to return from Madrid and declare: 'Well, George, we've knocked the bastard off.'

What he could do—all he could do, he decided—was to capture images of the antipodes on paper.

He would find, and record, interesting spots of the earth's surface in New Zealand and then search for the corresponding spots on the other side of the world.

The result would be an extraordinary series of photographs accompanied by fascinating pieces of descriptive writing, and he determined this would be his expedition's goal—though 'fascinating' was not a word previously used to describe anything he had written, and his photography skills were from the Instamatic Age.

To put his abilities to the test, one Sunday afternoon he took the family Nikon, set it on Auto, and drove into central Dunedin to experiment.

For his first interesting spot on the earth's surface, he settled on a plaque in the footpath in front of the city's distinctive railway station. The plaque depicted a Scotsman and a Maori. He took the photograph from above and labelled it his 'centrepiece'.

He then turned his attention to the view around him. While the railway station took up almost 180 magnificent degrees, the back end of the Cadbury's chocolate factory made the other 180 degrees less than perfect.

He took the photographs anyway and recorded the position on the Garmin Etrex global positioning satellite device he had bought for just a couple of hundred dollars from a little electronics shop in a Dunedin backstreet.

The first part of the experiment had been relatively simple, but with the limited knowledge of what he was doing, it now took him weeks to find, on a map, the approximate location of the antipodes of this first place.

The final answer was provided by internet website http://www.zefrank.com/sandwich/tool.html which showed that the antipodes of the plaque outside the Dunedin Railway Station was a spot in the Bay of Biscay, off the north coast of Spain.

At first, El Líder was disappointed, but the more he studied the distant bay, the more he marvelled at this whole new dimension to Dunedin—the city's connection with a bay containing nine species of whale, including the pygmy sperm whale; a bay across which the Spanish Armada had sailed; a bay that was the last resting place of scores of German U-boats, and the source of Spain's famous anchovies.

He suddenly had a yearning for the sharp, salty taste of anchovies and La Campaña added them to her shopping list for two weeks, until the yearning faded.

El Líder had not yet decided how or when he would introduce his wife to her expedition title but he felt La Campaña had a more companionable look to it than the more technically correct La Encargado. And it also had the exotic squiggle over the 'n'.

El Líder's internet explorations soon revealed that not only Dunedin was beyond the Spanish mainland. All the antipodes of New Zealand south of about Christchurch were at sea, in the Bay of Biscay, including such landmarks as Mitre Peak, Mount Cook, and his own suburban home.

Discouraged but not put off, he continued experimenting with ways to record places in a photographically interesting way. When his railway station photographs came back from the chemist, he arranged and rearranged them to produce a kind of 360-degree mosaic of that place's best features.

His plan was to find a series of such places across the New Zealand countryside. Perhaps twenty, he thought. Twenty Perfect Places.

These would be the most interesting and beautiful 360-degree views New Zealand had to offer. And in the middle of each would be a centrepiece of very high curiosity value. A plaque perhaps. Or a colourful rock. Or a native shrub. He dreamed of a cow pat—surrounded by black and white cows—in a green paddock—under blue skies. That sort of thing.

2

CANTERBURY

At the beginning, some expedition members were not even aware that they were on an expedition. They thought that the long, dreary hours staring out the window of the expedition bus were just part of a summer holiday trip to the top of the North Island. El Líder had mentioned his antipodean project in passing—but there had been so many projects over the years that no one had paid a great deal of attention.

At some point on the trip north from Dunedin, El Líder calculated, the expedition had crossed from the antipodes of the Bay of Biscay onto the Spanish mainland. He did not know exactly where the coastline was, but knew that Timaru was opposite the sea and Christchurch opposite the mainland, and that made Christchurch's Square a good place to start. It would be the expedition's first Perfect Place.

He strolled around the Square, scanning the ground for something interesting. Unfortunately, it was covered with paving stones made of concrete. As a centrepiece, he finally settled on a brass plaque set in concrete under a shady tree. It celebrated the arrival of the four ships that brought the first European settlers to Canterbury in 1850, but more importantly it gave him a view of the cathedral, the tram, and the chalice—the city's 18-metre-high, metal ice-cream cone.

El Líder wanted his photographs of each Perfect Place to be filled with people—typical New Zealanders doing their typical

New Zealand things. He lurked in the shade, waiting for interesting passersby, but the best he managed was a hurrying woman with a pushchair in the middle distance.

Eventually, he had 24 frames of THE SQUARE, CHRISTCHURCH, and returned to the expedition bus.

All the internet would tell him about the antipodes of Christchurch was that it was near the Spanish seaside town of Foz, a surfing destination where horse races were held on the beach during the summer. Foz was in the region of Galicia, which had 1,000 rivers, 'magnificent' beaches, 'beautiful' fishing villages, a stretch of cliffs known as 'the coast of death', and remnants of Celtic and Gaelic culture.

It was not much information, but it was a start.

Next stop on the search for pleasant 360-degree views was at the end of the New Brighton Pier where, conveniently, there were plenty of people preoccupied with baiting hooks and taking photographs of each other. El Líder chose the big yellow 'No Fishing' sign on the concrete deck as the centrepiece for FISHING OFF THE PIER, NEW BRIGHTON, then moved the expedition on to the Canterbury Plains.

He looked at Oxford's main street from every angle but could not find a Perfect Place, and spent quite a few minutes inspecting the Rangiora bandstand in the gardens before deciding it would not do. Then, on the outskirts of Sheffield, he stopped suddenly and studied the view west: an excellent panorama of snow-covered hills. He drove round and round the town looking for the place with the perfect 360-degree view.

El Líder had once flicked through a book of Robin Morrison photographs and felt that Sheffield's railway station—with its weathered sign and bullet-holed window—had the perfect, iconic, small-town New Zealand look about it.

The Square, Christchurch.

He used a railway spike as the centrepiece and was well satisfied with RAILWAY STATION, SHEFFIELD, CANTERBURY.

The day ended at Hanmer Springs where El Líder had in mind a Perfect Place in one of the hot pools. But when it came time to buy his ticket and take his camera inside, he began to have doubts. He had a vision of a steamy pool fogging his lens but, worse than that, he could see fellow bathers looking suspiciously in his direction as he took their photos.

He could imagine a lifeguard hauling him out of the pool and he could imagine a scene where he was required to explain his actions, but he could not quite imagine how his explanation was received.

He stood outside the pool complex in two minds for quite some time then, as a compromise, he recorded the pool's GPS position so he could search out its antipodes in Spain. If that proved to be an interesting place, he could return another day for the photographs of HOT POOLS, HANMER SPRINGS.

The explorers set up base camp at the camping ground—their tents tucked away on a pleasant, grassy slope handy to the ablutions block—and after a cup of black tea and a dry biscuit, they set out on a late afternoon walk in the sunshine, alongside a small stream.

El Líder strolled thoughtfully. He was disappointed with his lack of resolve at the pool and felt it betrayed his lack of confidence in the whole expedition.

He wondered if he might not just quietly forget it and revert to holiday mode. It could be easily done. Only he would notice.

They turned off the track into the Hanmer township to complete a circuit back to base camp and, by chance, they passed the Rustic Café.

El Líder stopped and read a message scrawled in chalk on the café's sidewalk blackboard. It was a Ralph Waldo Emerson

Railway Station, Sheffield, Canterbury.

quotation and it read: 'Do not go where the path may lead, go instead where there is no path and leave a trail.'

The explorers resumed their stroll, El Líder mulling over Emerson's quotation, and the more he thought about it, the more remarkable he thought it was.

Someone at the Rustic Café had chosen to copy that very quotation onto the blackboard on the very day he happened to be passing by with his mind full of expedition doubts. Extraordinary.

He reminded himself that, as far as he could tell, he was going where there was no path and, in addition, his notes and photographs might well be regarded as the trail he was leaving.

He was suddenly quite invigorated and wondered aloud if the expedition should have tea at the Rustic Café. La Campaña, however, had expedition supplies in the back of the bus she wanted to use up, so they continued on to the camping ground.

La Campaña cooked eggs, and beans in the expedition billy, and served them up with bread and salad on plastic plates in the gloom outside the camp kitchen. El Líder, with his hand around a warm bottle of Speights, breathed in deeply and smiled.

The expedition headed north-west in the morning, arriving at Murchison in time for lunch. Instead of joining the queue at the hot and crowded local café, they chose to picnic on a small, shady hillock in the grounds of the primary school, and congratulated each other on their good sense as they sat down on the soft, dry grass.

El Líder gazed through the heat haze towards forest-clad hills then turned his attention to lunch—watching idly as La Campaña prepared sandwiches with tomato, lettuce and capsicum, and filled plastic mugs with warm lemonade.

A wasp crawled under a lettuce leaf on one incomplete sandwich and then—moments later—a second wasp. El Líder alerted La Campaña who casually slapped one to death with the back of her hand.

The surviving wasp, startled, flew up into the air and dive-bombed El Líder—hitting his chest with a thud.

He unleashed a flurry of blows to the air in front of him and leapt to his feet. The wasp disappeared and he sat down again gingerly, expecting to be stung at any moment.

La Campaña found an ant in the chilly bin. Then her brow furrowed more deeply. The cheese was missing. As she continued to rummage, she recalled the disappearance of the yoghurt at one camping ground and the milk at another.

El Líder suggested that the dairy food thief might be responsible, but no one laughed, and he bit carefully into his cheeseless sandwich.

An angry thrush hopped about on the grass in front of them, impatient for them to finish so it could peck up the crumbs.

The sun went behind a cloud and the wind blew chilly.

El Líder gulped down his plastic mug of lemonade and inside ten minutes the expedition was back in the bus and on its way—El Líder forgetting in the rush to search Murchison for a Perfect Place.

Before leaving home, El Líder had begun putting together what he referred to as his 'expedition bible'—a blue folder of useful pieces of information for 'A Journey to the Ends of the Earth'.

Having been so impressed by the wisdom of Waldo Emerson, at the first opportunity he searched the internet for more quotes and added a second Emerson quotation to the 'bible'. 'Finish each day and be done with it. You have done what you could; some blunders and absurdities have crept in; forget them as soon as you can. Tomorrow is a new day; you shall begin it serenely and with too high a spirit to be encumbered with your old nonsense.'

El Líder felt it was a quote that could be useful one day.

3

NELSON-MARLBOROUGH

The expedition set up base camp on the south bank of the Opawa River in the Blenheim Bridge Top 10 Holiday Park.

The ground was soft and the grass was lush which was a relief to El Líder who had only his thin rubber sleeping mat and his thin down sleeping bag.

In the morning, low nimbostratus hung over Cloudy Bay as the explorers crawled out of their tents onto dewy grass. The weather was cold.

For breakfast there was Budget margarine—the price of Meadowlea at the local dairy beyond the ken of La Campaña. El Líder frowned at his toast and sipped powdered coffee from his plastic mug.

The morning's goal was to find a Perfect Place at Lake Grassmere where most of New Zealand's sodium chloride was produced, and the expedition bus was soon on its way.

La Campaña sat with a tourist map on her lap, and south of Seddon instructed El Líder to turn left onto the gravel of Blind River Road.

They wound their way through burnt, dusty hills onto flats of new, green vineyards. Most likely Sauvignon Blanc, said La Campaña.

They passed between two brown hummocks and when they

emerged, El Líder got his first view of Lake Grassmere. Immediately he stopped the bus.

Through the windscreen he studied a straight and desolate gravel road lined with power poles that drew the eye into the centre of the great, watery, salt plain where a small hut rusted picturesquely.

Here, amid the hundreds of hectares of shallow evaporating ponds, was exactly the photographic opportunity El Líder was looking for.

He grabbed his backpack containing camera, notebook, GPS device, toothbrush, previously-worn-but-not-yet-laundered underpants, T-shirt, and a variety of Australian coins.

Swinging out of the bus, shading his eyes against the glare, he announced that he was ready to go and that he might be some time.

He strode to the edge of a shallow creek separating the road from the salt lake and cautiously stepped into the shallows. The footing was firm. He took another step and again the footing was firm. He lifted his gaze from the creek to the photographic task ahead and took another step.

His front foot plunged into a quagmire of black ooze. His second foot followed the first and in an instant he was up to his chest in ooze—a filthy dark-chocolate mousse with no apparent bottom.

El Líder prostrated himself across the surface so he would not sink any further, then slithered and kicked to the far side and eventually flopped onto firm ground.

Expedition members laughed loudly from the bus as El Líder clambered to his knees and then his feet.

Barely pausing and with barely a backward glance, he made off towards his intended photograph, black from neck to toe.

Finding an interesting lump of powdery white rock, he carefully extracted the Nikon, using just his fingertips, and began

Lake Grassmere hut under grey skies.

taking photographs. The white rock would be his centrepiece and the scene around him would be LAKE GRASSMERE HUT UNDER GREY SKIES.

Still wet and black, he returned to the bus by way of a nearby culvert, washed as best he could in a stagnant stream, and drove the expedition off towards base camp. Along the way there were sniggering and complaints about the smell. El Líder wound down the windows.

He showered and applied lemon and lime shower gel, then joined the other expedition members for lunch of fresh bread rolls with cheddar cheese and tiny pieces of thin ham from the camp dairy.

The explorers discussed the second series of photographs they planned to gather that day — ideally a 360-degree, perfect view that would coincide with one of Marlborough's best-known wineries, like Cloudy Bay, for instance. El Líder liked the name and La Campaña had led him to believe it was quite famous.

But Cloudy Bay was a disappointment to El Líder as he steered the expedition bus up the driveway, through the tidy rows of vines. Approaching the winery buildings, he found them all too ordinary for his purpose, and he barely bothered to brake as the expedition swept past the frontage.

Allan Scott's Winery across the road was little better suited, although El Líder found the iron gates briefly tempting, and down the road, Hunter's overhead trellised vines were interesting but hardly of noteworthy proportions.

Dark clouds loomed over every horizon as El Líder led the expedition across the plains to HIGHFIELD ESTATE WINERY, BLENHEIM, which he had seen in a tourist brochure and hoped might prove to be a Perfect Place.

He brought the expedition bus to a halt below the winery. The explorers pressed their faces to the bus windows and peered up through the late afternoon gloom at a large building set high on the crest of a hill overlooking the plain. Highfield.

The countryside was still. The explorers waited. Silent. The expedition bus ticked as it cooled.

Suddenly, El Líder's mind was made up. It would have to do. He grabbed his backpack, handed the wheel to La Campaña and requested time alone.

La Campaña drove around a corner and parked out of sight on a grass verge to enjoy the last of the sunshine.

Minutes passed.

She heard the sound of footsteps in the gravel.

El Líder was at the window, requesting that La Campaña hand him the Fuji 200 ASA film he had left in the glovebox.

Returning to the Perfect Place, he loaded his camera.

A large red, ride-on mower that on their arrival had been mowing the road verges at some distance was now much closer. Its whirring blades and the sound of flicking stones added tension to the occasion.

El Líder surveyed the scene. He was looking for a centre-piece—an interesting shape; a small landmark in itself—that could be photographed easily from above.

There was only a farm mailbox. If it had been old, quaint, or unusual it would have suited El Líder's purpose well. But this one was shiny and new.

In addition, the land all around was flat so he could not get enough elevation to photograph the mailbox from above. He snapped it anyway, from head height, and turned his attention back to the 360-degree view.

On the hill in front was the great, brown winery with its tower glowing in a pool of pale sunlight. To the right was a narrow bridge over a dried-up, willowy creek, and to the left a narrow road and the large red mower.

El Líder waited for the dark shadow of a cloud to leave the winery.

As he lifted his camera for the first photo, from over the narrow bridge came a second mower.

It was smaller than the first but very fast-moving. It swept off the road and without pausing tore into the expanse of grass verge directly between El Líder and the winery. It darted rapidly back and forth in front of him.

Judging that by careful timing he might just manage to photograph the winery between the mower's sweeps — and urged on by the fading light — El Líder raised his camera and squeezed.

Nothing. No click. No whir. Again. Nothing. Again. Again. Again. Nothing.

A flashing light in the viewfinder indicated that the battery was low. It retained enough power to make the battery light flash but too little to make the shutter click.

El Líder extracted the two CR2-size lithium 3.0 watt batteries from the camera and rubbed the ends thoughtfully, in the hope that cleaner contacts might help.

They did not and he wondered why modern cameras needed small battery-powered motors to open the shutter and move the film along when a finger and thumb had done the job quite adequately for so many years before.

The bigger mower to El Líder's left was close now. It began to rain. El Líder packed his camera away and walked back to the expedition bus.

Dark and deflated at the Blenheim chemist shop, he asked the assistant why two such small batteries should cost so much but she did not appear to hear the question.

With the photo opportunity lost, El Líder steered the expedition bus back to the wet tents at base camp and began setting up for a wet night.

Highfield had not been the only failure in the northern South Island. The expedition had also not managed to conquer Mount Tapuaenuku in the inland Kaikoura Range.

El Líder's enthusiasm for 'Mt Tapi', as climbers referred to it, was to do with the diameter of the earth.

It had occurred to him that if New Zealand and Spain were on opposite sides, then maybe they also had the two most distant points on the planet, and he reasoned that of these two points, one would surely be at the top of a New Zealand mountain.

As Mount Cook and the other Southern Alps were off the map of mainland Spain, the next highest mountain, Tapuaenuku, had to be it, and the summit would be a Perfect Place.

At 9465 feet or 2885 metres, this climb was a relatively 'easy walk up in summer', according to an opinion El Líder had read on a website during the planning phase of the expedition, and from the comfort of his lounge, he had judged the climb an interesting challenge.

But the more imminent the opportunity became, the more daunted he was.

Calculating that to climb almost three kilometres vertically would be quite a long distance along the slope of the hypotenuse, he tried to compare the likely effort with something he was more familiar with—like the uphill route to his local dairy. But, then, he always took the car.

And, as well as the three vertical kilometres to the top, El Líder had not overlooked the need to walk all the way back down again.

The internet site claimed that 'only in winter' were ice-axes and crampons required on Mt Tapi, but El Líder felt there was always the risk of an unseasonal snowfall in the mountains and therefore the expedition's lack of crampons must be an issue.

And besides, the idea of the climb had been somewhat ruined for him by http://www.crystalinks.com/earth.html which found fault with his reason for wanting to do the climb in the first place. 'The Earth's shape,' the site proclaimed, 'is that of an oblate spheroid, with an average diameter of approximately 12,742 km. The rotation of the Earth causes the equator to bulge out slightly so that the equatorial diameter is 43 km larger than the pole to pole diameter... Due to the bulge, the feature farthest from the center of the Earth is actually Mount Chimborazo in Ecuador.'

To El Líder, the 'equatorial bulge' meant that pursuing the summit of 'Mt Tapi' would serve no real purpose, and the more he thought about it, the more he felt it could be left for another day, or even to another explorer.

The wisest course, he decided, was to find lunch and drive to Nelson where the expedition had on its agenda another climb — this one to the centre of New Zealand.

From a starting point in a flat, green park on the edge of Nelson, the explorers were required to follow a narrow pathway that twisted and turned upwards for about a quarter of an hour until, at the summit, they came to a monument erected by the Jaycees.

Various signs explaining the main features of the impressive view did not go into how this point was judged to be the centre of New Zealand but, nevertheless, it was now the Perfect Place for CENTRE OF NEW ZEALAND, NELSON.

El Líder often found himself being side-tracked as he pursued antipodes on the internet.

Nelson's antipodes, for instance, was somewhere in the Portuguese district of Bragança — a rugged, sparsely populated region near the Spanish border which, for 300 years, provided Portugal with kings.

In addition to that royal connection, it was in this region that Catherine of Bragança was born and she became the consort of England's King Charles II. And although she and the 'Merry Monarch' left no legitimate heir, before he died, Charles acknowledged 14 illegitimate children.

Two of them were Princess Diana's ancestors and that not only

Centre of New Zealand, Nelson.

gave Prince William a direct link with the beheaded Charles I (Charles II's father), but more importantly in the context of the expedition, it gave this hill overlooking Tasman Bay a link with the future King of England!

He noted too, that Bragança was regarded as a rural area in decline, a region where villages were being abandoned, the population was growing old, and rural schools were closing.

The day the explorers were due to leave their Blenheim base camp and cross to the North Island, it was raining. La Campaña swept out the tents with the new brush and shovel from the Two Dollar Shop and bundled the wet nylon loosely into the back of the bus alongside a few provisions that were still dry.

The expedition was booked on the Cook Strait ferry to Wellington, though El Líder could not remember at what time. He had made the booking by internet several weeks earlier and been given a special code number.

He had known that if he arrived at the ferry terminal without the code number there would be trouble of some sort so he had printed it and put it in a safe place.

In fact, he had printed it three times over several weeks when earlier copies put in safe places could not be found. He had also keyed the code number into his cellphone but, unfortunately, his cellphone had been in the pocket of his shorts during the black ooze incident and no longer worked.

One damp A4 copy of the print-out had survived but to El Líder's amazement, though it had the code number, it did not have the check-in time and ferry departure time.

He was tempted to ask Toll Shipping why these crucial details had not appeared but did not have the energy or, indeed, the phone.

He decided that 11 o'clock had about it the feel of a ferry departure time he might have booked and, having finished packing, pointed the expedition bus out of the Top Ten's front gate.

The driver's seat was still wet and a little smelly from the encounter with the black ooze and, as well, a damp towel had been left on the back of El Líder's seat.

Hunched over the steering wheel, peering through misty windows at the rain-swept highway, and with a large truck-and-trailer unit just a metre or two behind, he sped towards Picton.

They arrived at the ferry service's vehicle assembly point in good time for an 11 o'clock sailing. There was no ship and there were no other vehicles present. At all. And there were no staff in the ticket booths, either.

It reminded El Líder of the time when the Griswolds arrived at Wally World and found it closed. He recalled on that occasion a great deal of tension and someone making threats with a gun.

With no sign of a timetable and no one to ask, El Líder drove off through the steady rain to the information centre in Picton where his good humour was restored by simple answers to simple questions. 'One o'clock,' he repeated, just to be sure.

The coffee at a nearby café called Le Café cheered him further. He gave it a seven out of ten and the vegetable and cheese muffin nine out of ten. La Campaña made a note.

He picked up another Perfect Place, WATERFRONT, PICTON, because it was just over the road from the café. Then, having chosen coffee and photography over being first in the ferry queue, at the proper check-in time the expedition found itself at the end of a long line of cars idling in the rain. And by the time the expedition bus was on board and the explorers had reached the ferry's lounges, all the best seats were taken. El Líder spent the voyage outside in the scattered showers, scanning the shores of Tory Channel for interesting features. There were none that he could see.

He chose a spot at random in Cook Strait that might pass as a Perfect Place, and reached for the Garmin Etrex in his backpack. Its

Interisland ferry, Cook Strait.

battery was low so he joined a queue at the ship shop and shuffled slowly towards the counter. The attendant said she had run out of AA batteries. Was there anything else?

He went back up on deck, put the old batteries back in, and found they had enough power to mark one more Perfect Place. He then took photos of the sea and the sky and the ship and its passengers, and recorded in his notebook the coordinates for INTERISLAND FERRY, COOK STRAIT.

The antipodes, he found later on the internet, appeared to be near the Trabancos River—a tributary of the much more substantial Duero River, and known for its concentration of great bustards and for the largest reproductive concentration of black-bellied sandgrouse in Castile and León.

Eventually, the ferry backed in to the terminal at Wellington and the explorers headed below decks to the bus and drove onto the North Island.

4

FROM WELLINGTON NORTH

La Campaña suggested they find an interior Perfect Place for a change, and that led them to central Wellington's oldest building—the Colonial Cottage in Nairn Street.

They were greeted there by a young woman who was the guide and, because the cottage's credit card machine was broken, she offered the explorers a free tour on the proviso they did not let on to anyone else.

They were led into the small, two-storey building by the guide and three young helpers—ten-year-old girls from the neighbourhood who, it soon became clear, knew every inch of the cottage right down to the contents of the antique pencil case in the out-of-bounds territory beyond the yellow ropes.

The couple who built the cottage had had ten children and El Líder felt it was a shrewd move by the cottage's current owners to encourage three children to add life to what might otherwise be no more than a dreary old cottage.

Their enthusiasm for the tiny front room, upstairs bedrooms, wash-house and scullery distracted El Líder for a time but, after considering the options, he chose the kitchen as the most Perfect Place and asked the guide if he might remove the yellow ropes temporarily. Without fuss, El Líder was left to get on with INSIDE COLONIAL COTTAGE, NAIRN STREET, WELLINGTON.

On the trek back to the expedition bus, El Líder struggled to

Inside Colonial Cottage, Nairn Street, Wellington.

keep up with the pace being set by La Campaña. Weeks of sandal-wearing had created painful cracks in his heels, and while uphill walking was fine, the walk down even the gentle decline of Willis Street was agonising.

He suggested La Campaña go on without him. But she refused, and slackened the pace a little before calling a coffee break as they approached Starbucks.

El Líder had once had a bad Starbucks experience during a visit to Rotorua, so insisted on coffee at nearby Smith the Grocer instead. La Campaña judged the coffee there a little bitter, but El Líder added sugar as usual and did not notice.

The expedition returned to the car park at the 'cake tin' — just six dollars for a whole day — and El Líder contemplated the potential for a series of photographs from inside the stadium.

He pictured the kick-off point on the halfway line just as Daniel Carter kicked off, with the All Blacks spread out on one half of the field and the Australians on the other — and the Bledisloe Cup somewhere in between. It would be the Perfect Place for KICK-OFF POINT, 'CAKE TIN', WELLINGTON!

But, in case it proved difficult to arrange, he sought out other Perfect Places around Wellington, eventually settling on the downtown view from SHORELINE PLAQUE, OUTSIDE THE BEEHIVE, WELLINGTON.

The expedition headed north under cloudy summer skies. It was too hot inside the bus for El Líder, and too cool outside.

It was some consolation knowing that in the high, inland Castilla region of Spain — where Wellington's antipodes lay — the temperature in December averaged four degrees Celsius and that one winter minus 27 degrees Celsius was recorded there.

Castilians were apparently fond of saying, of their climate: *'nueve meses de invierno y tres meses de infierno'* — 'nine months of

Shoreline plaque, outside the Beehive, Wellington.

winter and three months of hell' — the 'hell,' no doubt, summer temperatures above 40 degrees Celsius.

In contrast, El Líder noted that he often said of New Zealand's climate: '*Realmente no puedo tomar más de esto*' — 'I really can't take any more of this.'

The explorers reached for their jackets and stepped out into the breeze to add THE EIGHTEENTH HOLE, TITAHI BAY, WELLINGTON, to their list because that was the golf course where U.S. Open champion Michael Campbell learned the game.

They also stopped at Titahi Bay itself, where the colourful boatsheds helped turn the rugged, friendly little bay into a Perfect Place, and a small shrub struggling to survive on top of a rock next to the sea provided the perfect centrepiece for GREEN SHRUB AT TITAHI BAY, WELLINGTON.

They continued up the coast, pausing briefly for SAND DUNE, PARAPARAUMU, KAPITI COAST, and then made for Stonehenge.

This was a place El Líder had a particular interest in using as a Perfect Place because it promised from its centre an interesting view through all 360 degrees.

The expedition arrived at Masterton too late to book a henge tour for that day, so moved on to the camping ground where the camp 'host' advised them that 130-kilometre per hour winds were expected during the night and that all the camp's campers had moved out as a precaution. He warned them not to pitch a tent.

La Campaña's first preference was always a tent but in these circumstances she was willing to consider a cabin. El Líder's first preference was always a modern hotel but he joined La Campaña to take a look inside one of the cabins.

With the camp host hovering nearby, they pushed open the door. They looked and sniffed and decided they would take their chances with the tent.

Titahi Bay, Wellington.

Sand dune, Paraparaumu, Kapiti Coast.

After studying possible sites from various angles, they settled on a spot well away from power lines and tall trees, and reasonably sheltered from the weather.

There were no other tents.

They parked the expedition bus strategically to help protect them from the storm, El Líder banged in all the tent pegs he could find, and the explorers crawled inside to wait for the worst.

Rain and wind rattled the tents violently throughout the night, according to La Campaña. El Líder heard nothing worth waking for.

By morning the storm had passed. Base camp was unscathed so La Campaña went for a swim while El Líder waited for the tents to dry before packing them into their bags.

Each time they were almost dry, a short shower swept through until, finally, El Líder bundled the whole soggy, nylon mess into the back of the bus. He slammed the boot and the clouds parted and the sun shone powerfully.

They left Masterton in good time for the early afternoon tour of the henge. They were passing through the Wairarapa's wine-growing region, although wineries were not on El Líder's itinerary.

At the Gladstone Winery, the expedition began veering off course. La Campaña's 'quick look' became an interminable discussion with the cellar door person. El Líder had downed a couple of early vintages on arrival and soon lost track of the conversation, wandering aimlessly in and out of the winery while La Campaña calmly swirled, sniffed, sipped, and spat her way through the entire selection.

When eventually they left, El Líder had a bottle of Sauvignon Blanc under one arm and a light head. He decided for the sake of other road users to skip the tasting room at the next winery. And the next.

The morning rolled on pleasantly enough, El Líder the only

one anxious that they not forget the day's real destination.

La Campaña had three tourist maps and a road atlas laid out in the front seat along with two large water bottles, handbag, newspapers, brochures, and assorted clothing. She also had, in her head, the complex directions to the henge, given to her by the previous cellar door person. There were no signposts; the new henge business was still waiting for the engineer from the local council to return from his holidays to approve their installation. With just minutes to spare, the expedition finally found the henge on a hill overlooking the plains of the Wairarapa.

El Líder's anxiety at being late was gradually overtaken by boredom as they waited on the arrival of other lost people with bookings for the 1.30 p.m. tour.

Henge expert, Richard Hill, told them that whole tour busloads of henge visitors had gone missing on previous occasions because of the lack of signs and El Líder wished the engineer bad weather on his holidays.

He handed over ten dollars for each expedition member, then Hill led them into the henge and began to slowly drown them in information—a tour de force of hengology, astronomy, astrology, navigation and religion.

It was an extraordinarily generous performance and El Líder believed he had never before received so much wisdom for so little money. After two hours, La Campaña felt the same and retired to the expedition bus for a rest.

El Líder drove away from the henge desperate to remember what he had been told and frustrated that, an hour later, he was certain only that the Virgin Mary was not a virgin in the modern sense of the word, but for the life of him he could not remember how anyone could tell that from the array of concrete rocks that made up STONEHENGE, NEAR CARTERTON.

Stonehenge, near Carterton.

Ekatahuna. El Líder stopped in the town's main street because he liked the name. At first glance through the expedition bus's rain-splattered windscreen, Ekatahuna seemed an unlikely location for a Perfect Place. It was wet, it was cold, it was windy, and this was summer. They were parked outside the public toilets in the empty main street.

El Líder bought the explorers a chocolate Trumpet each and they ate them silently, sheltering under the verandah of a closed shop with a Takeaway sign. In the window were sun-bleached stuffed toys, irrigation systems for gardens, a large wooden toy train, and some copper seahorse mobiles, but no sign of any takeaways.

El Líder contemplated the rain and low cloud for a long moment, wondering what to do next. He could not invent Perfect Places. He could only find them. And in Ekatahuna he did not know where to start looking.

The easiest course was to give up, and back in the bus he waited for expedition members to join him, swung out onto the road, and accelerated towards the edge of town.

But just as the 100 kph speed sign beckoned, he had an urge not to give up. He swerved off the main road and hunted the expedition bus through some side streets. A few blocks, a few turns, a string of weatherboard houses, and El Líder suddenly stopped the bus in the middle of the road.

He leapt from the driver's seat—La Campaña not far behind—and craned his neck over a locked gate at the entrance to the town's bowling green. Down one side ran a neat row of white-painted bench seats. At the back there was a splendid pavilion and on the other two sides, colourful flower beds and mature specimen trees.

El Líder could imagine taking photographs from the centre of the rink of bowlers dressed in white. A Perfect Place. But not today. The green was empty. He grasped his GPS device and

Windmills, Palmerston North.

carefully recorded the coordinates in his notebook and, happy now, drove off through the rain, imagining the day he would return for EKATAHUNA BOWLERS IN THE SUN.

The expedition continued northwards. El Líder was keen to find a Perfect Place in Palmerston North and was drawn towards the view of some windmills on the edge of the town. But although he found an interesting tree stump to use as a centrepiece, and found the slow-twirling windmills against a dark sky impressive, the other 180 degrees had limited appeal.

It was a pity because he knew that part of the expedition's work in Spain would involve exploring Don Quixote's La Mancha, and any windmill connection with New Zealand would be especially relevant.

Standing on the stump, his hand shading his eyes, El Líder stared up at the windmills. He could not see how they could be mistaken for giants, but expected Spanish windmills would be different. He hesitated, then took the photos anyway for WIND-MILLS, PALMERSTON NORTH.

Almost by accident, he stumbled on a Perfect Place a few kilometres south of Palmerston North, at Shannon. It was in the centre of the town's rugby ground, and although it was not the 'cake tin' and there were no All Blacks in view, he took photographs of the ground from the muddy centrepiece and left quite satisfied with KICK-OFF POINT, MOYNIHAN PARK, SHANNON.

Like much of the southern half of the North Island, Shannon appeared to have its antipodes in the region of Castilla y León which covered a high, inland plain dotted with medieval castles.

This provided El Líder with another chance to connect New Zealand and Spain, in this case via a colourful poem by Margaret Mahy about a 'foolish and old' King of Castile and a remarkable bottle of wine which '… tasted of phoenixes, tasted of flowers /

Kick-off point, Moynihan park, Shannon.

It tasted of summer-time's happiest hours…'

Ms Mahy had to be referring, El Líder deduced, to either Henry the Infirm or Henry the Impotent—two of the 25 kings of Castile—and the bottle could only have been the famous Castilian wine from the grape Tinto Fino, responsible, according to the internet, for both 'fruity young' reds and 'complex, alluring aged' reds. El Líder was willing to accept that his theory was a good one but that it might, nevertheless, be completely wrong.

At Dannevirke La Campaña suggested they stop for tea in the rain, so El Líder carried the chilly bin through the late afternoon gloom to a seat and table under a little roof next to a playground.

They had reached Dannevirke after passing through kilometres of picturesque green hills that La Campaña suggested looked quite perfect enough to her. El Líder explained that picturesque was one thing but a Perfect Place required something more and only he had any idea what that might be. And even he did not always recognise what that something was.

Dannevirke was a fine example. El Líder knew that the antipodes of Spain's capital city, Madrid, was near Dannevirke, but was not aware, until the expedition stumbled across it, that the town had a Madrid Street.

He stopped the bus underneath the sign of that name and walked along the footpath to view the street from various angles.

Aside from its name, it was a most ordinary street, and he suspected that if any Madrid Street residents emerged from their homes they would be ordinary New Zealanders. But no one emerged. El Líder noticed, through a window, that *Coronation Street* was on.

For the life of him, he could not think how to make photographs of this street interesting. It was just too ordinary and he climbed back into the expedition bus and drove off.

It was only months later that he realized he had missed an opportunity, failing, as he had, to recognise that MADRID STREET, DANNEVIRKE, was a Perfect Place just because it was so ordinary.

Madrid Street, he found, was opposite Ciempozuelos — once a village and now a suburb 30 kilometres from central Madrid.

The expedition arrived at Havelock North ready for its Hawkes Bay campaign, and set up base in the motor camp. The next morning, El Líder and La Campaña rose early and set out on a walk through the town's neat, freshly painted suburbs.

They passed a cheerful, grey-haired early-riser trimming his edges and, near the Summerset in the Vines Retirement Home, a group of grey-haired, pastel-clad walkers who said good morning politely.

El Líder and La Campaña were in a hurry, anticipating the imminent arrival of another expedition member. But at the critical point where they were required to turn left, back towards camp, an attractive suburban hedge of grapevines distracted them. From there on, every step took them further along the road to Matua Peak Winery, and further from camp.

As the houses grew sparser and the vines predominant, it became clear that a mistake had been made. As they retraced their steps, they discussed the origins of the mistake and concluded that neither should accept the blame.

Back at camp, the newest member of the expedition dumped his bag and his laptop at the rear of the expedition bus, sat down to breakfast of boiled eggs on toast, and began a complex software conversation with another expedition member. El Líder listened for a time and then drifted off to wash the breakfast dishes.

Hawkes Bay's antipodes were in the part of Spain El Líder felt was the most potentially eccentric — the region the internet described as the 'autonomous community' of Castilla-La Mancha where Don Quixote had his encounter with windmills.

El Líder had opened Miguel de Cervantes' famous book several times over the years, seriously intending to read the whole thing, and such was his enthusiasm for the gaunt, shambling, deranged Don that he had included in the expedition bible part of that most famous chapter:

> ... and as soon as Don Quixote saw them he said to his squire, "Fortune is arranging matters for us better than we could have shaped our desires ourselves, for look there, friend Sancho Panza, where thirty or more monstrous giants present themselves, all of whom I mean to engage in battle and slay, and with whose spoils we shall begin to make our fortunes; for this is righteous warfare, and it is God's good service to sweep so evil a breed from off the face of the earth."
>
> "What giants?" said Sancho Panza.
>
> "Those thou seest there," answered his master, "with the long arms, and some have them nearly two leagues long."
>
> "Look, your worship," said Sancho; "what we see there are not giants but windmills, and what seem to be their arms are the sails that turned by the wind make the millstone go."
>
> "It is easy to see," replied Don Quixote, "that thou art not used to this business of adventures; those are giants; and if thou art afraid, away with thee out of this and betake thyself to prayer while I engage them in fierce and unequal combat."
>
> So saying, he gave the spur to his steed Rocinante, heedless of the cries his squire Sancho sent after him, warning him that most certainly they were windmills and not giants he was going to attack. He, however, was so positive they were giants that he neither heard the cries of Sancho, nor perceived, near as he was, what they were, but made at them shouting, "Fly not, cowards and vile beings, for a single knight attacks you."

El Líder hoped the expedition might encounter these same wind-mills one day, but the first task of the day was to find a Perfect Place in Havelock North. El Líder had in mind a roundabout he had seen near the town centre but, on returning to take the Perfect Place photographs, he saw that the flowers of the potential centre-piece were a shade less brilliant than before, and the boulevard of green and gold trees lacked its earlier lustre.

He climbed back into the expedition bus and announced that he intended not only to give up on Havelock North, but would also skirt the city of Hastings; he declared that he had been there once and it had nothing to offer.

Fifteen minutes later, as a result of confused signage at a roundabout, the expedition bus was in the heart of Hastings, where the streets were full of happy Christmas shoppers and hundreds of cheerful hanging baskets. A fountain played in the centre and, nearby, two entertainers sang and played guitars.

Parking the expedition bus on yellow lines in a nearby car park, El Líder took only moments to capture BRONZE SCULPTURE, HASTINGS, and after that, Napier's sculptural offerings were almost an anticlimax.

He inspected the cleverly constructed art deco tribute to the officers and crew of the *Veronica*, and the nearby reflecting ball, courtesy of the friends and family of Percy Spiller, and decided that they had the 360-degree credentials. But wait as he might, El Líder could not seem to wait long enough for something to happen on the broad expanse of concrete.

There were pedestrians in all directions but none came close enough to give this Perfect Place the human element he wanted. He began to suspect that it might have something to do with his own lingering presence so, eventually, snapping off his roll of film, he accepted that REFLECTING BALL OVERLOOKING THE SEA, NAPIER, was another place that might require a second visit.

Bronze sculpture, Hastings.

Reflecting ball overlooking the sea, Napier.

The fuel light in the expedition bus had been on empty for quite some time. La Campaña wanted to stop only at Shell service stations because each fill of diesel earned at least two Fly Buy points. But the last Shell sign El Líder had seen was in the rear view mirror, on a busy street, where a U-turn seemed impractical. So once again they were at Mobil.

La Campaña was increasingly interested in the expedition's finances and in particular the tax advantages of collecting receipts. El Líder was not entirely certain where the taxable income might come from—publishing deals and movie rights still some way off—but he felt that with a potential market of four million New Zealanders plus 67 million Spaniards and Moroccans (not to mention Portuguese and Gibralterians), publishers, television producers and, ultimately, the IRD, would be beating a path to his door.

La Campaña had grown skeptical of such speculation during other ventures, and El Líder decided to keep this part of the plan under his hat for the moment.

Each morning for a fortnight, the explorers—after showers, toast and coffee—rolled up their tents, sleeping bags and general paraphernalia, and left it all at the rear of the expedition bus for El Líder to pack. His primary object at packing time was to keep all components instantly available so as to satisfy any whim of any member of the expedition. El Líder's greatest fear was that an item packed in the wrong place in the morning could lead to a major 'unpack-repack' later in the day.

The lessons in conversational Spanish were a case in point. La Campaña had gone to some trouble to obtain books and tapes so that as the expedition progressed, the driving time could be spent learning the language. But early every morning El Líder inadvertently packed the Spanish tapes at the bottom. And later every morning, once they were on the road, La Campaña wanted the language material. And every day El Líder was forced to think up a new excuse to avoid the 'unpack-repack' scenario. The result was that after a fortnight's travel, the sum total of new Spanish learned was, '*¿Dónde está el baño?*' or, 'Where is the bathroom?'

With just six months to go until the Spanish leg of the expedition was due to begin, El Líder felt a growing urgency over the language issue, but this sense of urgency never seemed to coincide with each morning's packing of the bus.

La Campaña suggested that perhaps they should attend a series of Spanish classes when they returned from their current excursion, and El Líder felt he had no choice but to be enthusiastic.

Leaving Hawkes Bay, the expedition enjoyed a morning without rain, though the expedition bus's lack of air-conditioning became more apparent as it ground its way into the hills through a hot, dry wind. Near Taupo the wind turned cold and it began to rain. They wound up the windows and breathed a little easier, though their good humour, already wilted by the heat, plunged with the cold.

La Campaña insisted they stop to eat the lunch she had packed in the morning, so El Líder swung off the highway into the access road to the Huka Falls. Disgruntled explorers trudged through puddles along the one-minute walking track to look at the falls for a moment before settling at a wet picnic table covered in bird droppings.

A mob of sparrows descended, hovering to take pieces of La Campaña's lunch from between the explorers' outstretched fingers.

A brown hen with an aggressive stance and an insane look in its eye barged into the sparrow throng and also demanded to be fed. The explorers obliged for a time but, receiving no sign of gratitude from sparrows or hen, soon resumed eating the lunch themselves.

El Líder had looked at the falls and judged them too difficult to photograph in a way that would produce 360 degrees of interest. But as he leaned on the safety rail and gazed, a jet-boat full of tourists sped upstream and into the churning water beneath the falls. El Líder recognised that the Perfect Place for JETBOAT AT HUKA FALLS, TAUPO, would be on board the boat.

He wondered how much it would cost to take the trip and he weighed up his chances of getting all the photographs he needed on just one trip. Perhaps it would be wise, he decided, to first find out what was on the other side of the world. El Líder sometimes became ensnared by La Campaña's limitless frugality. But only for brief periods.

On checking the internet, he felt that the antipodes of Huka Falls held some promise, lying, as it did, just outside the village of Santa Elena (pop. 1000) situated in the remote, mountainous north of the Jaén province of Andalusia, and surrounded by olive groves.

The Waitomo Top 10 Holiday Park was idyllic in the late afternoon sun — its grass green, its trees shady and its toilets spick and span. El Líder rolled on his Ultraguard Insect Repellent and contemplated the purpose of his visit. He had thought it would be an interesting variation to get his next photographs inside a limestone cave.

After setting up base camp, the expedition drove to the Waitomo Glow-worm Caves ticket office where La Campaña paid for an 8 p.m. tour — earning at the same time an 80 percent discount on the entrance fee for the Museum of Caves, which would now cost the entire expedition just one dollar. The cave tour was to include some underground walking followed by an underground boat ride.

La Campaña decided at the outset that she would secure the front seats in the boat so that expedition members would have the best possible, uninterrupted view of the glow-worms hanging from the ceiling.

The guide was called Kiwi. The other members of the 8 p.m. tour were an American man from Abu Dabi, an American woman from Alaska, their two American teenage children, and a wealthy extended family of Indians led by a thickset, middle-aged man immaculately dressed in black, white and gold, whom one expedition member dubbed 'the man with a million questions'.

Kiwi was a pleasant, patient Maori of about 20 with a carefully rehearsed patter meant to carry the group smoothly from one point of interest to the next. But 'the man with a million questions' could not wait for the orderly dissemination of cave information and had extracted from Kiwi much of his cave knowledge even before the group had gone inside.

Each of Kiwi's answers was rapidly translated for the non-English-speaking members of the Indian party. They descended into the caves. A stream of questions rang out. The information flowed from Kiwi. And the Indian party nodded solemnly as 'the man with a million questions' translated. The caves were full of noise.

As the group moved amongst interesting limestone formations, La Campaña's focus was firmly fixed on being first in the boat. Where Kiwi went, La Campaña followed like an eerie shadow: around the stalagmites, into 'the cathedral', past 'the organ pipes'.

El Líder began to sense that the Indian party had the same intention as La Campaña. A kind of underground chess game was being played—the Indians and La Campaña attempting to checkmate Kiwi. La Campaña was outnumbered five to one (and outweighed ten to one) but stuck to the task, sliding into each new cavern in good position.

El Líder—a distant pawn—was finding the tour rather tiring. Along with the natural splendour of the scene, there was the ceaseless interrogation of Kiwi, the rapid-fire translation, and the tense manoeuvring for boat seats.

Finally, Kiwi announced the boat ride. The Indian group coalesced into one body—the three men and two women moving in perfect unison to block La Campaña at the last bridge.

La Campaña was beaten by better teamwork and El Líder wondered if he could have done more.

But the game had not yet been played out. At the boat, Kiwi took control of the boarding and, as anyone who has been on the Waitomo Glow-worm Caves boat trip will know, those at the front of the queue go in the back of the boat.

So, as Kiwi pushed off into the inky darkness, the dawdling Americans had the pleasure of riding at the front.

La Campaña took this as a victory of sorts and *ssshhh*ed the Indian man who continued to talk against the advice of Kiwi as the boat drifted into the glow-worm-lit grotto.

By now, the real purpose of the expedition's visit to the caves had slipped El Líder's mind. He had only realised after the tickets were bought that taking photographs in the caves was not allowed but there was an even bigger problem. El Líder's GPS device would not detect satellites from underground. So El Líder emerged from the caves not only photoless but without a GPS position. He slumped on a rock next to the portaloo, recorded the less-than-Perfect Place, JUST OUTSIDE THE CAVES, WAITOMO, but took no photos.

The expedition added GOVERNMENT GARDENS, ROTORUA, and continued northwards—thoughts of Cape Reinga drawing El Líder on—though he had not yet mentioned this ultimate goal to

Government Gardens, Rotorua.

expedition members already incredulous at the time it was taking to reach Auckland.

El Líder planned to find a Perfect Place in the Bay of Plenty but somehow the turn-off was missed. No one on board knew whose fault this was, though all were certain they were not to blame. El Líder suggested that, much as he would like to do the driving, and the map-reading, and the watching out for signposts all by himself, even he required a little assistance sometimes late in the day when the sun was in his eyes.

The village of Omokoroa happened to be the nearest place an expedition approaching the Bay of Plenty from the south, and which missed the turn-off after a long day on the road, would find a camping ground, and that's where base camp was set up for the night.

El Líder could find no Perfect Place but enjoyed an early morning walk to the beach and up through the Captain Crapp Reserve.

He arrived back at camp with his heart set on a leisurely soak in the smallest spa pool in the camp's three-pool complex and was disappointed to find that an elderly woman with a wrinkly brown face and perm was already in his chosen pool.

Politely El Líder eased himself into the larger, empty pool nearby and began reading the *Property Press*, hoping to discourage conversation. The previous evening he had been trapped in the kitchen for a very long time by a Dutch couple determined to describe to him every climatic similarity between New Zealand and the Netherlands and he wasn't falling into that trap again.

As the elderly woman headed home after her hot soak, she stopped at El Líder's pool and began discussing Omokoroa's wet and windy summer. He sighed to himself and responded politely. The conversation moved on quickly through the state of Omokoroa's real estate market and the village's growth, to what was really on the woman's mind—the tragic death of her father on the family farm at Penrith in Cumbria 70 years earlier.

Her father had been in a concrete shed with his best bull—an animal with a ring through its nose so it could be led from one insemination job to the next. This day, the bull became agitated and struck her father, flinging him about the pen and up against the concrete walls.

The woman was just six. She saw what was happening and ran for help. Her brothers waded in with pitchforks but that only enraged the bull further. Then the farm dog attached itself to the bull's nose and that turned the tide.

Her father never walked again and was bedridden until he died.

The woman finished telling her story and announced that she must go home and clean her windows.

El Líder was left soaking thoughtfully in his pool, pondering the relevance of this story to his expedition.

Before leaving home, La Campaña had baked a large Christmas cake to take to Auckland, and El Líder had found a secure place for it in a box amid the luggage in the rear of the expedition bus. The cake had travelled safely for several days until La Campaña, herself, upset it by turning it on its edge. This was bad enough but to avoid further damage it was decided to leave the slightly battered cake in one of the tents at Base Camp Omokoroa during a sortie to Mount Maunganui. When the expedition returned, La Campaña crawled into the tent containing the cake and made an unhappy discovery. She saw one cockroach and suspected that there was a second. There was no obvious sign that anything had been harmed or that the cockroach had come into contact with the cake. But from that moment on, the cake's reputation was sullied in the minds of La Campaña and El Líder. The question was: should anyone else be told?

It was not quite Christmas, but it was the summer solstice. El Líder had begun paying more attention to the earth's cycles since the henge tour. It dawned on him that if it was the longest day of the year in the Bay of Plenty then it would be the shortest day in Jaén, the Andalusian province at the Bay's antipodes, which one internet site rated as the world's biggest producer of olive oil.

Other sites described what the Spanish were doing while El Líder mooched around the campsite. The people of Jaén were particularly enthusiastic about winter solstice bonfires or *hogueras* which they jumped over as a symbolic protection against illness. And the winter solstice was marked by the drawing of Spain's national lottery called *El Gordo* — The Fat One.

The visit to Mount Maunganui had not been a success. El Líder had in his mind a 360-degree view of the Mount's beach with a centrepiece of gently rolling surf.

The beach was empty when the expedition arrived; a howling wind was sending sand blasting along the water's edge.

El Líder parked the bus with a view of the beach, but no explorers offered to step outside. El Líder watched a cloud of sand engulf the long, spindly legs of the surf life-saving tower and reached for his backpack. He decided not to take his camera or his notebook — only his GPS in its moulded-rubber, shockproof case.

He staggered through the sandstorm to the sea, removed his sandals and tested the temperature. This would be far enough. With the sand stinging his calves below his board shorts, El Líder shielded his eyes against the sandstorm and took a reading in the hope that one fine day he would return for the photographs he needed for THE BEACH, MOUNT MAUNGANUI.

5

AUCKLAND

The explorers arrived in Auckland in time for Christmas and everyone put the expedition out of their minds, except El Líder. On a previous trip to Auckland he had photographed and recorded an assortment of Perfect Places as an experiment, but because he had written the GPS positions on a scrap of paper and then lost the scrap of paper, he had no option but to revisit them all.

He could make no headway on Christmas Day, but found an opportunity on Boxing Day and persuaded a reluctant group of barely interested explorers to join him on a sight-seeing trip into the city.

He managed to get as far as AUCKLAND TOWN HALL, QUEEN STREET, where he recorded a new GPS position but by now the barely interested had become the openly hostile, and El Líder and La Campaña were alone as they tacked past the Viaduct Basin to WATERFRONT SCULPTURE, AUCKLAND, to complete the excursion.

El Líder returned to the expedition bus, satisfied at having suffered nothing more than a bad coffee and an eight-dollar parking fee.

El Líder was determined that one Perfect Place would be a beach. Mount Maunganui had been a failure so, while exercising along Takapuna Beach on Auckland's North Shore, he was on the lookout for gentle waves washing onto the sand that he could use

Auckland Town Hall, Queen Street.

as a centrepiece to go with a nice 360-degree view.

It was an easy place to find and where the beach-front homes were at their most impressive, he waded into the surf until the waves were lapping at his knees and his shorts were wet at the bottom, and set about taking the 24 photos that he devoted to each Perfect Place.

After two or three photos, La Campaña pointed out that this particular expedition film was the one that had been used during Christmas Day festivities. El Líder looked down at the counter. A long walk, in the midday heat, without a hat, would be required to obtain a new film.

El Líder did own a hat.

For the first two weeks of the expedition he had not required it but knew exactly where it was packed, in the event that the sun suddenly came out. And now that he needed it, it was gone.

It reminded him of the stick of insect repellant that had gone missing on this expedition the night of the attack of the mosquitoes, and of the annual disappearance of his sunglasses in the days leading up to a holiday.

He suspected that the hat had been moved by an expedition member, but could not make up his mind who or why. Dark thoughts swirled around him as the sun beat on his head through thinning hair, but as he splashed his way through the shallows of Takapuna Beach, in the general direction of a chemist shop, his mood improved rapidly—as it always did on a beach.

The walk progressed into the streets of Takapuna where the explorers felt that more than just film was required. It was lunchtime and they were thirsty.

El Líder had a new credit card which worked fine as a credit card but would not produce cash from a cash machine or do Eftpos. La Campaña had suggested several times that he visit a Westpac Bank branch to get the problem fixed. But he had delayed because he suspected he would need i.d., and his wallet, containing all his i.d., had not been seen for several days.

So now the explorers faced shops selling cold drinks that would not take the credit card, and a photographic shop that would take the credit card but did not sell cold drinks.

El Líder felt sure that all their money problems would be solved at the Westfield Mall but La Campaña—who had not objected to walking the beaches of Takapuna in bikini top and shorts—was now too modest to enter the mall.

El Líder explained shortly that there was no alternative, and carved a path through the throng of happy shoppers into the heart of New Zealand consumerism and found that, even here, a can of Coke could not be bought with a credit card.

He was prepared to go without. But La Campaña was not. She approached a supermarket specializing in Asian food and service, and soon returned with drinks and sticky sesame bars which they consumed in a glass-sided bus stop for want of anywhere better to sit.

El Líder returned to his spot in the surf and trained his camera on interesting features around him.

Little children ran into the waves. El Líder got them. A woman with a hat swam past. El Líder got her.

After a few minutes, La Campaña waded in to the sea to join him—concerned that the subjects of El Líder's photographs, or their parents, might soon begin to question his motives. El Líder suddenly felt conspicuous.

A wave hit him in the back and salt water splashed across his camera. That was enough. He dried the camera as best he could with the driest part of his shirt sleeve and left with TAKAPUNA BEACH, AUCKLAND on film.

Takapuna Beach, Auckland.

The rest of the day, the explorers sunbathed and swam and watched boats and people drift through the heat and calm of an Auckland summer afternoon. So enchanted were El Líder and La Campaña with this Auckland beach that they stopped at a small camping ground next to the sea, called Takapuna Beach Motor Camp, and enquired about setting up base camp there.

Tents were erected in moments and beds laid out. La Campaña marvelled at being given a key on a string for the ablutions block—the expedition's first encounter with such exclusivity.

But some of the explorers were tiring of camping grounds. Sleeping in a small tent flapping in the wind, surrounded by the sounds of jandals slapping by, and happy children running and shouting, was not the issue. It was the stainless steel kitchens, the pokey concrete-block showers with their clingy nylon curtains, and the cramped toilets with their devices designed to make the theft of toilet paper difficult.

Worn down by these hardships, on a gloriously hot beach day, one expedition member announced that this was the end for him and he was going home just as soon as someone arranged his flight and paid for it.

El Líder and La Campaña suggested that he might like to make the arrangements himself—finding a train, perhaps, and a ferry and a bus. They drove the grumbling expedition member to the Takapuna information site and waited on a yellow line in the midday heat. The cost of the flight, it transpired, was quite similar to the train-ferry-bus option, but with three hours in the air instead of three days on the road.

El Líder found it hard to argue and offered his credit card so the ticket could be bought on the internet, but the expedition member explained that the card was not necessary as he had memorised its numbers on a previous occasion. El Líder felt the need to say something but could not think what.

They drove to the domestic terminal where the departing

explorer climbed out, slung his bag on his back, adjusted the headphones of his i-pod, and with a final, 'Yup', when reminded to feed the cat and water the plants, sloped off into the terminal, homeward bound.

Crossing the Auckland Harbour Bridge a few days later, El Líder thought he saw the makings of a Perfect Place — a yellow building with a red-tiled roof on a rocky point opposite the city. A glance at the map suggested the point would be at Devonport, but on arrival there, it was obvious that it was not. La Campaña suggested that Devonport might do — picturesque as it was — but it was not the point El Líder had in his mind.

They could not find the building but by now were at the Bayswater Marina and El Líder was distracted by new possibilities. Somewhere amongst the marina's rows and rows of expensive-looking boats and kilometres of floating boardwalks, he was sure he would find a Perfect Place. But his heart sank when he saw that each boardwalk was guarded by a heavy, metal gate complete with a slot for a plastic card.

He studied one of the gates carefully. It was designed to be difficult to climb. The alternative, he thought, would be to approach the marina from the harbour, by boat or by swimming. He imagined black, oily water and the smell and taste of salt and diesel. He sat in the bus, drumming his fingers on the steering wheel. No one spoke.

After several minutes, El Líder climbed out and approached the gate for a closer look. At just that moment, a man carrying tools walked past him, swung the gate open and walked through.

El Líder seized the moment and caught the gate before it closed. He stepped through and sauntered down the boardwalk — determined not to appear suspicious by looking back over his shoulder. He followed the workman at a distance, expecting at any moment that the man would turn and stop him, or that someone would shout. But the workman ignored him and no one shouted.

La Campaña had been lagging behind and had missed the opportunity to slip through.

El Líder stopped at the first line of boats and watched as she approached the boardwalk gate. The workman and his mate were kneeling down applying a spanner to a metal object. Their backs were to the gate. La Campaña pushed at the gate. It swung open, having not been locked in the first place. El Líder was slightly disappointed. He waited for her to catch up and they set out towards the marina's outer breakwater, passing between rows of boats. But the further they went, the more obvious it became that the boardwalk did not connect with the breakwater, where they expected the best view of the city, and they were soon on their way back through the gate.

Nearby they found a sign inviting members of the public to walk along the breakwater — the sign complete with tips on how not to fall into the water. When they reached the end, El Líder studied the 360-degree view dominated by the shining city across the harbour and the dark-grey silhouette of the harbour bridge. He was well satisfied and used up a lot more film than he had planned to — La Campaña contributing by insisting on photographs of El Líder and expedition members at the Perfect Place, BAYSWATER MARINA, ACROSS THE HARBOUR FROM AUCKLAND CITY.

The region corresponding with Auckland was Andalusia, a large chunk of Spain stretching northwards from the Mediterranean, which had not only a long, complicated history from the Tartessian Empire, through the Vandals and Visigoths, but also a preponderance of bullrings — 70 in all — and a very full calendar of fights during the season. El Líder took note that it was bad luck to wear yellow to a bullfight and that a matador's satin 'suit of light' was trimmed with gold.

Bayswater Marina, across the harbour from Auckland city.

And, according to the guidebook El Líder had been given for Christmas, Andalusia was the home of flamenco, and a region overflowing with fresh fruit, fine hams and good sherry.

The expedition returned to Devonport and a Mexican restaurant which the explorers approved of for its salads and décor, although El Líder felt that his flat-white suffered from too little coffee and a touch too much milk. He gave it a five, which La Campaña felt was ungenerous, and after idling through a shop full of New Zealand art, and streetside stands of cheap books, the expedition headed back to base camp artless and bookless.

As El Líder prepared to leave the Auckland segment behind, he received a bonus. One expedition member wanted to visit the famously iconic west coast surfing location of Piha Beach which was not on El Líder's list of possible Perfect Places.

They had no map of West Auckland but headed west expecting to pick up a sign to the famous beach.

Signs, however, did not appear in any of the many streets the expedition passed through although El Líder felt, from the position of the sun and the general topography, that they were heading in approximately the right direction.

La Campaña suggested El Líder ask directions but the opportunity to stop never arose. She began looking out for cars carrying surfboards but no cars with surfboards were seen, suggesting that wherever it was they'd spent the lost hour in West Auckland, it was not near the road to Piha.

When they did arrive, the day was gloomy and the wind was messing up the waves for the few surfers in the distance but, for better or worse, El Líder scratched 'Piha' in the sand and photographed the centrepiece for BETWEEN THE FLAGS, PIHA BEACH, AUCKLAND.

Between the flags, Piha Beach, Auckland.

6
NORTH OF AUCKLAND

Lying on the warm, dry grass outside the tents at Takapuna base camp, El Líder had time to consider the next leg of the expedition—the push for Cape Reinga. He felt it would perhaps be best if he went alone. This would save the remaining expedition members hours of travel and, by all accounts, though a pretty enough place to drive through, the north had mosquitoes and black sand on its beaches.

Morale was never high on El Líder's expeditions so why risk it, he thought.

The importance to the expedition of reaching Cape Reinga could not be overestimated. It would settle the question of whether New Zealand's antipodes stretched as far as the mainland of Africa, as El Líder hoped, or veered off into the Atlantic Ocean.

The day finally came. El Líder was up before the sun. He started the expedition bus and drove off quietly through rows of darkened tents and campervans. He was equipped with a full tank of diesel, road map, cash and credit card.

Over the next 17 hours he would circumnavigate Northland, arriving back at the Takapuna Beach base camp exhausted but with a dozen Perfect Places under his belt: Dargaville, Opononi, Rawene, Ninety Mile Beach, Cape Reinga, Kerikeri, Waitangi, the Bay of Islands, Pahia, Kawakawa and Whangarei.

He would flop into his tent and fall instantly asleep.

Among his most prized Perfect Places was Tane Mahuta, the giant kauri tree he had found towering over a gallery of tourists in the Waipoua Forest.

El Líder always left his camera on Auto, aware that Manual required mystical decisions about light and speed. This time, though, he suspected that Auto would not cope with both the very bright sunlight on Tane Mahuta and the darkness of the surrounding vegetation.

The Auto solution was to pop up the little flash on the top of the camera in a bid to light the entire scene. El Líder was skeptical but kept his thoughts to himself. It would be weeks before the non-digital film was developed and he would know if Auto was right or wrong.

Tane Mahuta, and the lighthouse at Cape Reinga as well, held another challenge — how to get 360 degrees of pictures without upsetting the tourists.

It was easy enough to line up alongside dozens of others to take photographs of a tree or a lighthouse. But it was a different matter getting the other 180 degrees. It meant inhabiting the area between tourists and their photographic subject — a no-man's-land through which people normally scuttled, bent over and apologetic.

El Líder was finding it a very empty and lonely place, particularly when — his back to the landmark — he turned to face the tourist cameras and lifted his own camera to photograph them. He tried to think of a simple explanation but could not, and felt compelled to shoot from the hip surreptitiously, rapidly and randomly. It would be weeks before the results of this technique would be known.

And the whole business of being a lone tourist made him nervous, too. At each tourist spot he was the only one unattached. Tourists seemed rarely to come in ones.

But these were all minor issues. LIGHTHOUSE, CAPE

REINGA had done New Zealand proud. The sun shone, the wind hardly blew.

He had half hoped, on arriving there, to be a little unnerved at reaching the end of the land. But he wasn't. The northern tip of New Zealand was just one more place where the land ran out and the sea began.

More unnerving had been the 20 kilometres of winding, gravel road to the lighthouse. El Líder considered himself an expert on gravel, and he was not alone. A stream of cars and buses sped through a continuous dust-cloud, swerving and overtaking in a mad rush to the end of the country and back again to the bitumen.

With the expedition bus's windows up El Líder could hardly breathe for the heat. And with the windows down he could hardly breathe for the dust. To take his mind off the discomfort and to fill the time, he decided to sing. He began with 'Tie me kangaroo down sport, tie me kangaroo down...' which seemed appropriate in the heat and the dust.

But like a stuck cd player, he could not get beyond a few lines of that song, let alone move on to the lyrics of any other song. And weeks after his trip to the Perfect Places of the far north, he would still be haunted during idle moments by a cockatoo and an Australian called Blue.

But his visit to the north was complete. He had more Perfect Places than he could count accurately and was, in fact, a little muddled between those places he had photographed successfully, those he had photographed in part and would have to return to, those he had photographed but in retrospect considered less than perfect, and those he had not photographed but wished now that he had.

He hoped it would all become clear in time, and the expedition, having conquered New Zealand, went home.

PART
2

THE
OTHER END OF
THE EARTH

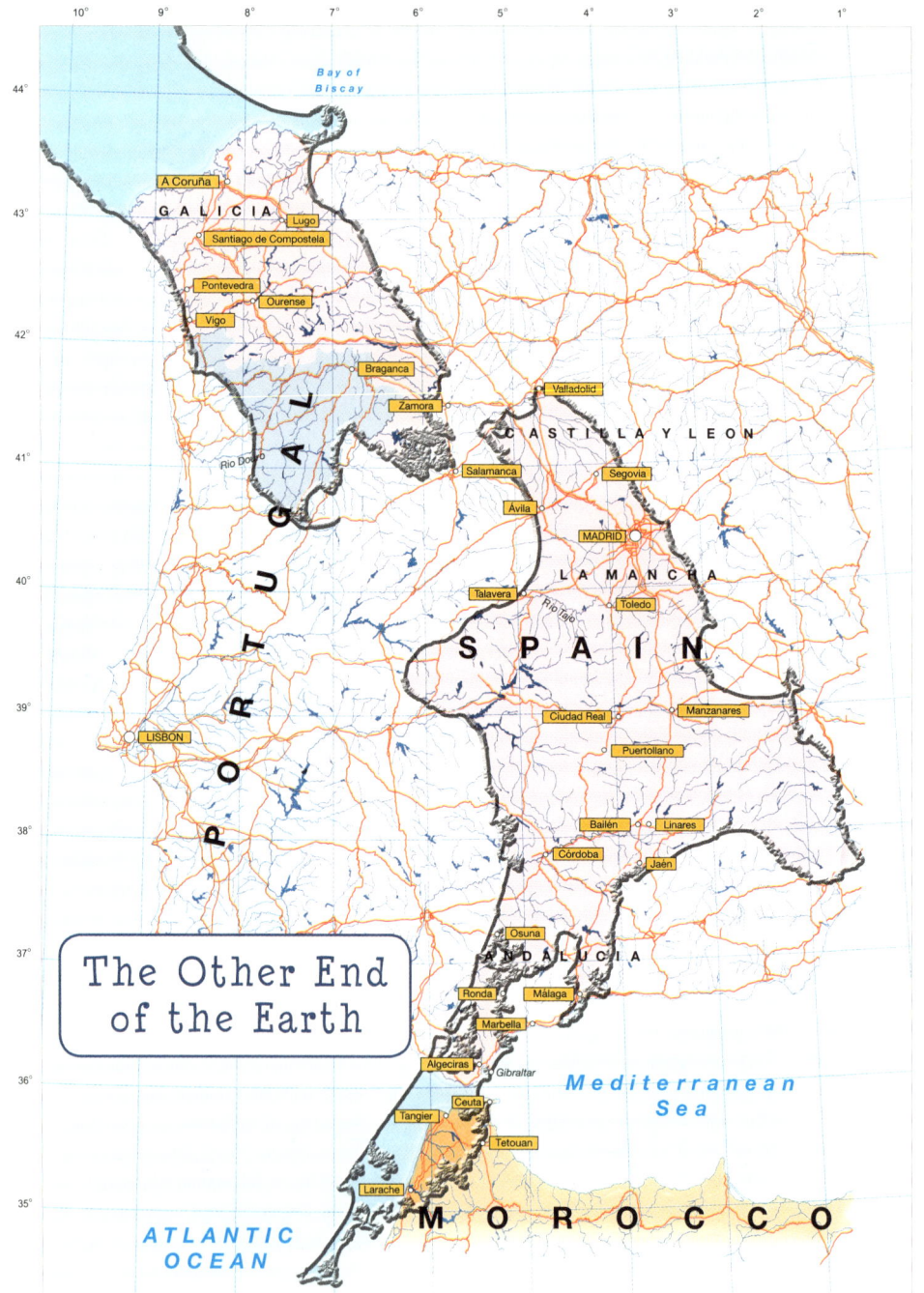

The Other End
of the Earth

7

GETTING STARTED AGAIN

Back home, El Líder devoted every spare moment to planning. Could they learn Spanish in six weeks? Would his credit card work in Morocco? Could he find his passport?

La Campaña produced the language video. The opening pictures were in black and white and from this and from the shape of the bikini on the young woman frolicking in the surf, El Líder deduced that the film was made in the early seventies.

There was no English translation or supporting literature. El Líder and La Campaña watched and listened mutely as waves of Spanish washed over them.

Foreign words never stuck in El Líder's mind for more than a day, and most for less than a minute. The video was not helping and he was resigned to the expedition being reliant on the Spanish nation's willingness to speak to them in English as they journeyed to the ends of the earth.

La Campaña found an Otago Polytechnic Spanish course and signed up all members of the expedition and one Thursday night they joined a dozen eager students sitting attentively around a U-shaped cluster of desks. It had been advertised as a class for beginners, but straight away El Líder noticed that some were not beginners at all, chattering among themselves in what he assumed must be Spanish. What were these people doing here?

He vowed to work hard at his Spanish homework, to give him a head-start the next week, but when they got home, he and other expedition members could not agree on the correct pronunciation of any of the written sentences and were completely thrown by upside-down question marks and r's that were meant to roll. And who knew what j's were supposed to do?

In between short-lived bursts of Spanish, El Líder explored the origins of the notion of antipodes. The internet led him back to St Augustine who was born in 354 AD and was now best remembered for being an antipodean sceptic. 'As to the fable that there are antipodes, that is to say, men on the opposite side of the earth, where the sun rises when it sets on us, men who walk with their feet opposite ours, there is no reason for believing it. Those who affirm it do not claim to possess any actual information; they merely conjecture…'

El Líder found himself being drawn into an internet debate about who had thought the earth was flat and who had not, and quickly decided to move on.

One of the tasks El Líder had been putting off was converting his New Zealand Perfect Place GPS coordinates into their exact antipodean equivalents. The Garmin Etrex displayed the degrees, hours and minutes of latitude and longitude south and east. EKATAHUNA BOWLERS IN THE SUN was, for instance, S 40° 38'45.3, E 175° 42'31.5.

El Líder had never dealt with the technicalities of navigation before and was uncertain now about his ability to accurately convert these complex strings of southern hemisphere positions into their northern equivalents. The first part of the calculation — to get the latitude — required him to take the S and change it to an N. That part he had no problem with. But finding the longitude required more than just a change from E to W. An internet site told him to subtract the E number from 180 degrees which might have been reasonably simple except that some of the numbers were degrees, some were minutes and some were seconds.

El Líder's head hurt.

He rang a yachtie to check the methodology and he also returned to the GPS shop to double-check his calculations. If he was right, the antipodes of EKATAHUNA BOWLERS was N 40° 38'45.3, W 4° 17'28.5 and that was somewhere in Spain. And if he was wrong—well it did not bear thinking about.

El Líder's planning got a major boost when an expedition member pointed out to him the antipodean map site zefrank.com. In a matter of hours he had found in Morocco and Spain the antipodes for all the points he had gathered througout New Zealand over the previous three weeks.

Unfortunately, he soon discovered that the antipodes of Cape Reinga, Tane Mahuta, Rawene, Opononi Beach, Ninety Mile Beach and Dargaville lay in the Atlantic Ocean off the Moroccan coast.

These places were in roughly the position one internet site suggested the lost city of Atlantis might be, but that was of little consolation to El Líder who reluctantly erased them from the expedition's itinerary.

That left him with BRIDGE, KERIKERI, as his most northerly Perfect Place. El Líder had stopped there on his dash to Cape Reinga, and had a collection of photographs taken from the bridge that included a stone building and a genuine steamboat.

Kerikeri seemed small and beautiful but, as it was very late in the afternoon and he was there for less than ten minutes, he could have been wrong.

Its antipodes, he found, was on a hill, perhaps in a forest, inland from the northern Moroccan town of Larache (pop. 100,000) and close to the ancient ruins of Lixus, a town established by the Phoenicians 3000 years ago.

Bridge, Kerikeri, north of Auckland.

Lixus was where Hercules supposedly gathered golden apples in the gardens of Hesperides—the penultimate of his twelve labours—and El Líder learned from another site that Lixus had a wonderful view appreciated best with a picnic.

He also liked the internet descriptions of Larache's whitewashed houses with blue doors. 'There is a relaxed atmosphere to Larache, no hustling, lots of Moroccans with the best intentions in mind, little difference between the sexes. Social life in Larache is highly developed, with long mingling hours in the evenings.'

Larache, 87 kilometres south of Tangier, he decided, would be the expedition's base camp while it searched for the antipodes of Kerikeri.

The six-week trip to Europe had initially been planned as five weeks' holiday and one week of experimental antipodean exploring in northern Spain. But as time passed, the expedition expanded to take up most of the holiday. Six weeks seemed far too little time, in fact.

And to El Líder's consternation, as departure time loomed, expedition members offered their own ideas on where they wanted to go. La Campaña liked the idea of visiting beautiful and culturally interesting places in entirely the wrong parts of Morocco.

Marrakesh might well be interesting, El Líder conceded during a noisy discussion one evening, but it was a hell of a long way from the end of the earth.

After returning from the New Zealand leg of the expedition, El Líder had turned his notes into 'Journey to the Ends of the Earth, Part One' which he found to be an accurate and absorbing record, and he decided to send the unfinished manuscript to a publisher to test the water.

No matter what he tried, his computer would print only in single spacing, and although he knew full well that publishers with acres of print to read every day insisted on double spacing, he was in a rush and he sent it off anyway.

Unbeknown to El Líder, 'Journey to the Ends of the Earth, Part One', after passing through the hands of a less-than-enthusiastic reader, found its way to a shelf in the publisher's office and lay forgotten. Months passed.

El Líder's planning became sporadic and lethargic. The garden shed he was planning to build took up more and more of his expedition planning time. He stopped reading books about explorers and whereas he'd once surfed the internet with vigour, he now strolled on the beach.

La Campaña continued making travel arrangements — station wagon to Christchurch, plane to Casablanca, train then bus to Larache.

Larache would be the starting point from which the expedition would launch itself on an overland journey to the north coast of Spain — a trip that would mirror a New Zealand journey from Kerikeri to Christchurch.

But El Líder felt it would all be for nothing if a publishing deal was not struck — the expedition reduced to mere holiday status and the fascinating series of Perfect Place photographs reduced to a stack of lowly tourist snaps. With the departure time fast approaching, he rang the publisher. He assumed the long wait signalled a complete lack of interest. But he was wrong.

At a meeting in the publisher's office, he discovered lukewarm interest, or more accurately, interest that was a degree or two cooler than lukewarm.

His expedition in search of Perfect Places was likened to train-spotting.

'Well, carry on,' said the publisher doubtfully. 'If you think you want to.'

With only days until departure, and with much to do, El Líder became side-tracked by a library book that traced the trials and tribulations of fellow explorers like Christopher Columbus. Columbus had endured years of discouragement, derision and hostility over his plan to sail west from Europe. King John II of Portugal turned him down flat and, after years of delay, a special commission finally reported to Queen Isabella and King Ferdinand of Spain: 'We can find no justification for Their Highnesses supporting a project that rests on extremely weak foundations and appears impossible to translate into reality…'

El Líder was not sure how weak his expedition's foundations were but at least he was not relying on royal patronage for three ships and 90 sailors.

During the final hours of planning, he added last-minute details to what was now his 200-page expedition bible. It contained anything he could find that might help with the route he hoped to follow from Larache—including train timetables, lists of nice places to stay and notes on the Moroccan royal family, the Barbary pirates, the architecture of Santiago de Compostela, the Berber version of Islam, and the ancient art of *zellige* (or *zellije*).

Departure day minus one and the entire expedition was struck by illness. El Líder read of the same thing happening to David Livingstone. Livingstone had called his illness 'severe intermittents' and he suffered heart palpatations, vomiting, sweating and his urine contained 'much brick-dust-like sediment'.

El Líder had more the runny nose and the stuffy head and took Panadol.

He had expected the packing to be more fun; had seen himself in khaki shorts and double-breasted khaki shirt, carefully checking off provisions as they were stowed by bearers in the back of the expedition station wagon. (The expedition bus had unexpectedly expired after the exertions of Part One.)

El Líder discovered that some of the most admirable packing

ever had been carried out by Robert Burke and William Wills. When they set off from Melbourne to explore the interior of Australia, they took 27 camels, 23 horses, 37 guns, and 21 tons of baggage including 60 gallons of rum for the camels.

El Líder tried to work out a joke about rum and camels and duty free to tell La Campaña, but could not seem to get the words right.

His own packing was over almost before it began. One small backpack. One heavy tent. One bulky sleeping bag. One pair of sandals. Six white shirts. Some underpants and socks. Camera. GPS. Notebook. Pencil. Pencil sharpener. And, of course, tickets, money and passports.

In the modern way, El Líder's expedition would travel light—living off the land, accepting the hospitality of locals, sleeping under the stars—or paying by credit card where necessary.

Departure day and El Líder was ready to leave long before the rest of the expedition had finished breakfast. La Campaña insisted he clean the station wagon while he waited.

He calculated the distance to Christchurch airport against the time available and believed—as he watched expedition members gradually fill their backpacks—that it might still be possible.

Eventually, the station wagon was full and El Líder rolled down the driveway and out onto the street. He swung the wheel towards the antipodes and tried to clear his mind of the little things with which it was cluttered, and to see the big picture for a moment.

Here they were, on one side of the globe, the planet, the earth, about to travel to the other side. He took a deep breath of the southern atmosphere and exhaled noisily. In a moment they would be past the turning point and on their way.

The turning point was an intersection where El Líder traditionally turned back for the cat accidentally locked inside, the tap left on, or some item forgotten.

The station wagon passed through the intersection and El Líder began to relax. An explorer then remembered he had not brought with him the black tie that went with the cherry red suit he had worn at the previous night's school formal and had to return to the suit hire place that morning.

El Líder turned back for the tie, stopped at the suit hire place, and at last began to circle the earth towards the antipodes, by way of the road to Christchurch.

The Journey to the Ends of the Earth had begun.

Eleven hundred and eighty-seven metres above the earth and 1166 kilometres beyond Sydney, tea and coffee services were suddenly suspended. The pilot warned that he was expecting turbulence.

A large man across the aisle from El Líder continued to doze, a crying baby in the distance continued to cry, and on the tiny television screen a few millimetres in front of El Líder's face, Kath continued to model lingerie.

The pilot's name was David. He was American and he was a captain. His co-pilot was Ramesh. These details El Líder had picked up from the 'welcome aboard' message delivered just before take-off.

El Líder had asked an Emirates public relations person in New Zealand for permission to meet the men and women who would hold the lives of expedition members in their hands from Christchurch to Casablanca. He had questions that he felt entitled to ask. His request was referred to Dubai where it was refused.

El Líder could not imagine Magellan setting out to circumnavigate the globe without first meeting his helmsman and the rejection put El Líder's nose quite out of joint.

Now he was left with questions about turbulence but no answers.

For instance, how bad did turbulence have to be before tea and coffee services were suspended? And how bad did turbulence have to be before the wings broke off? Just two questions that came to mind.

Had he been given the chance to ask David and Ramesh about turbulence, he would have also slipped in questions about their level of experience and, for that matter, he would have been able to check them over for nervous tics and signs of recent drug use. And it would have been comforting to see inside the cockpit to ensure it was free of half-empty gin bottles and fast-food wrappers.

The turbulence amounted to a few brief vibrations and was never mentioned again by either David or Ramesh. The coffee arrived and El Líder returned his attention to *Kath and Kim*.

His plan had been for the explorers to assume Spain time from the beginning of the flight so they would suffer less from jet-lag. This was an idea he had picked up from a television travel show. But by 11 o'clock in the morning, Spain time—and before they'd even begun to cross the Great Sandy Desert beyond Alice Springs—the cabin lights had been turned out and all the expedition was asleep.

El Líder would have joined them but he had a case of the fidgets. There was nowhere that his feet were comfortable. His ankle hurt. Then his knee. Then his hip. Then his ankle hurt again. And he was hot. He thought of battery hens in cages and pigs in sow crates. He was tired but he could not sleep.

He listened to a few minutes of 'Still Air', flicked to 'Music for Yoga', then 'Glistening Beach' then 'Gentle Slumber' then back to 'Still Air'.

The Great Sandy Desert came and went. The baby that stopped crying only long enough for its batteries to be changed had finally fallen asleep — or been put to death — El Líder did not care which.

He tried a burst of 'Al Fatina' from 'The Holy Qur'an', and gazed restlessly about the darkened cabin.

The toilets did a steady trade. David and Ramesh roused sleeping passengers occasionally with announcements about seat belts.

El Líder had 500 movies and video clips at his fingertips. He laughed through the one episode of *Frasier* and three episodes of *Kath and Kim*, and smiled serenely through the opening song from *The Sound of Music*. Nothing else really appealed.

He wrote a few notes with Fat Freddy's Drop playing in the background: 'Ground speed 888 km/h. 10.12 hours to Dubai. Altitude 10,363m.' Then, unexpectedly, he fell asleep over the Timor Sea, leaving David and Ramesh to fly the plane alone.

At Dubai the Australian passengers left on connecting flights to Europe and the expedition joined another planeload of Arab and African passengers. The women were mostly dressed from head to toe in black. All carried huge suitcases disguised as hand luggage that they struggled to cram into the overhead lockers with the help of cheerful Emirates staff.

El Líder judged the African men to be traders of some sort, moving goods around the world with an eye for a slim profit. They were young and lean with flashing white teeth and they were busy and confident. One, El Líder noticed approvingly, wore 'Globetrotter' shoes.

With the change of plane, the explorers had moved from one world into another. They were now a small, pale Australasian enclave in a colourful, boisterous African world. There was more leg room but less padding in the seats.

8

ANTIPODES OF NORTH
OF AUCKLAND

They landed at Casablanca—a city of three million people, and the commercial power-house of Morocco, but irrelevant to El Líder, and the expedition went straight from the plane to the train that would take them to the bus for Larache.

For months, in his worst nightmare, El Líder had seen tired expedition members troop off a dilapidated bus into a dim and menacing desert town, the streets sometimes dusty, sometimes dark and shadowy. They would trudge from back-street hotel to back-street hotel until, finally, they would have nowhere to stay. He had tried and failed to visualise what happened next.

It did not help that he had read a warning about Larache. It was a town with little accommodation. Internet sites referred to 'decayed elegance' and 'faded' hotels, and the Lonely Planet guide said of Larache: 'Little visited and under appreciated, Larache has an unexpected charm in its tumbledown medina and Spanish fla-vour…'

El Líder was always wary of 'tumbledown'.

Four hours after leaving Casablanca airport, the expedition was still trundling through the Moroccan countryside by train. Clearly, it had failed to get off at the right station for the bus to Larache and no matter how fast, uncrowded and comfortable the train, it would not get them to Larache which was not on the rail network.

El Líder had left his map of Morocco at home to save weight and was struggling to come up with an alternative to the bus plan.

It was a relief when the decision was taken out of his hands eventually and everyone was required to get off the train at a town called Kenitra.

It was the middle of the afternoon. It was dusty hot. There were no maps in the small, dark railway station. There were no signs that mentioned Larache and there were no speakers of English. A tall, distinguished man in a suit tried to help in French. Two girls in robes and headscarves tried to help in Arabic. The man behind the ticket counter tried to help in sign language.

The afternoon ticked by. The expedition sat down in the empty station café and a waiter brought coffee and Danish pastries. Morale was low. El Líder expected criticism but the explorers were too exhausted. He thought back to his internet research and tried to visualise one of the maps of Morocco he had pored over. He could dimly remember references to a tourist town near Larache called Asilah which had its own railway station, and suddenly it became clear.

A clean bed and a hot shower in Asilah were all they needed, and the hot shower could wait.

La Campaña had the expedition's greatest grasp of French and went to buy the tickets while El Líder played with his cellphone. Before leaving New Zealand he had arranged with Vodafone for his phone to work in Morocco, but it seemed unlikely to El Líder that he would have the correct code or the correct pin number.

The only Moroccan phone number he had was for a Larache pension that had appealed to him. He pressed the numbers without hope, was startled when he heard the dial tone and flummoxed completely when someone answered.

Michel was the stand-in manager for Maison de Haute, Larache. He had arrived from Paris a week earlier and he had no more idea about where Kenitra was or how the expedition might get to Larache than El Líder did. But he pencilled in a booking for the expedition, wished El Líder luck, and hung up.

For three hours, trains came and went. Every time the expedition moved to board one, someone would be on hand to assure them this was not the train they wanted.

Expedition members could not seem to work out the timetable or the signs for themselves. They climbed on one train but a moment later—under advice—were off it again. Then, in a confused haze, they watched from the platform as the train they needed to catch arrived and departed without them.

Eventually, in the gathering dusk, tired and frustrated, they leapt aboard a train and settled in, determined to go somewhere, and for two hours they raced through the darkness—their destination a mystery.

The other passengers tried to speak to them in English and tried to help. Good-natured arguments broke out in Arabic between different groups of helpers over where the expedition should get off.

On one occasion the expedition climbed off the train onto a dark and empty platform, then hastily scrambled back to the security of their brightly lit carriage.

Towns and crossings flashed by. El Líder put his trust in a young Arab woman with an unruffled, educated, but non-English-speaking air. After many false alarms, she indicated that the time had come for them to get off and, finally, ten hours of train travel was over.

The expedition stumbled out of the station into the night and was caught up in a swirling melée of cars and people shouting and jostling cheerfully under patches of streetlight.

They had no idea what town they had arrived in but, ignoring the possibility of a comfortable bed, El Líder and La Campaña said to a tall Arab man in some way connected to the taxi industry: 'Larache.'

'Larache?'

On the train ride it had become clear that their pronunciation was wrong so they repeated the name, giving the syllables a different emphasis each time.

'La-rash, La-rarsh, La-raysh.'

They were soon in a battered yellow Mercedes *grand taxi*, hurtling along a narrow strip of seal in the dark—the back end so low under the weight of six passengers that the headlights irritated oncoming traffic.

Larache's streets looked dark and shadowy through the taxi's windscreen, but not dusty. The driver stopped at the *grand taxi* depot and professed no knowledge of where La Maison Haute was, nor any desire to go looking. El Líder had no intention of getting out of the vehicle until they were at the front door.

He rang Michel and handed the phone to the driver. There was a conversation in French and the taxi started off again into narrow streets crammed with people—the driver tooting politely to warn pedestrians not to take the fatal step into his path.

Michel was waiting for them in the town's crowded, but dimly lit, central plaza—Place de la Liberation—and led them down a dark alleyway, through a dark and noisy market, up dimly-lit, steep flights of stairs, and into a huge, four-room apartment with a high ceiling and an abundance of beds with firm mattresses and clean, cool sheets.

The expedition drank excellent tea from Paris and then slept.

The internet had explained that La Maison Haute was a charming Hispano-Moorish house set in the bustling *bab al khemis*.

Early the next morning, the expedition discovered what this actually meant. They were in the town's market square. And, while some vendors went about selling their chickens, fish, teapots and cloth quietly, those selling music cds used their sound systems as weapons to compete with each other. Three or four of the loudest were directly below La Maison Haute.

El Líder peered down on the market. It was a foreign and fascinating scene: men in immaculate white robes, women in aqua-blue and canary-yellow robes, young men in jeans and baseball caps—all shuffling along the cobblestones through the clutter of stalls.

Two men discussed a second-hand fridge, two neighbouring traders shouted at each other and waved their arms, and a woman walked by carrying under her arm a melon the size of a large rubbish bin. And not a western face to be seen. It reminded El Líder of a Hollywood movie set and he would not have been surprised to see Michael Douglas striding past on some American mission or other.

Breakfast was served on the roof with a view across the River Loukos to the Atlantic, and also across the roofs of whitewashed villas stacked with satellite dishes. They drank the sweetest, freshest orange juice and ate croissants and fruit. El Líder was especially taken with the Victoria plums.

An explorer still suffering from a New Zealand cold entertained La Campaña by recounting his night's sleep—the all-night barking dogs, the 4 a.m. call to prayer, the street chatter and cellphone ring tones at dawn and, finally, the all-eclipsing Arabic music from the sound systems of the market.

It astounded El Líder, as he gazed about him, to think that where he could now see chunky metal fishing boats promenading along the Loukos, he once would have seen wooden pirate ships of the 'Barbary Corsairs'. He had read a little of Barbarossa—or Red Beard—who commanded galleys rowed by British sailors and fishermen he had captured or bought in Morocco's slave markets. And he was fascinated, too, that this once lawless harbour in Morocco was at the antipodes of the once lawless Bay of Islands which one J. Bidwell in 1836 wrote, was "... notorious at present for containing, I should think, a greater number of rogues than any other spot of equal size in the universe." It was another rather slim connection, El Líder had to admit.

He drank his coffee and felt that here on the rooftop he could begin to recuperate from the nightmare journey so far, and should spend the day contemplating Larache from above.

But La Campaña had not come all the way to Larache to sit in the sun drinking coffee and sipping orange juice, and soon they were filling water bottles and backpacks for an attempt at finding their first antipodes—that of BRIDGE, KERIKERI.

The expedition flagged down a *petit taxi* in the plaza and asked to be taken to the ancient, ruined city of Lixus across the Loukos on a hill they could see from their rooftop garden.

As they drove towards Lixus, El Líder's GPS confirmed that the closer they got, the nearer they came to the antipodes of Kerikeri.

The expedition stepped out of the taxi, paid the driver, and made for the well-trodden path leading up the hill to the ruins.

El Líder was looking forward to seeing the remains of a Phoenician temple and a large mosaic of Neptune in the place where Hercules once gathered golden apples. But just metres along the path, he noticed that the digital arrow of the GPS was now pointing not towards Lixus but away towards a barren hillside of random goat tracks, long, dry grass and patches of thistles.

He paused. Lixus had been such a part of his planning that it was a shock to now consider not going there.

But there was no argument. With GPS held flat in his hand at waist height so he could see its arrow, he turned his back on Lixus and led the expedition off the path towards the thistles.

They did pass by some stone enclosures that El Líder assumed were the garum factories where the salty fish paste was manufactured for the Romans before the fifth century, but they did not stop and were soon at a sealed road with verges where they could walk easily.

El Líder's mood improved with every step. Habit and conditioning would have had them falling into step with the tourists trudging up the hill to the tourist site. But here they were instead, explorers, strung out along the edge of a noisy Moroccan highway; passing mysterious and unsavoury factories and derelict farmhouses without a clue about where they were, where they were going, or what they might find when they got there. And the further they went and the further away they got from the tourist trail, the happier El Líder became. He was so happy he could have whistled.

As he took in the dry plains and hills around him, he could imagine the marching armies of conquerors from Morocco's past — the Phoenicians, the Carthaginians, the Romans, the Vandals, the Byzantines, the Arabs, the Portuguese, the Spanish and the French. Now here were the New Zealanders.

After a few kilometres the road began to veer away from the antipodes of Kerikeri, so they turned onto a potholed side-road heading further into the countryside.

They passed a man on a donkey cart and a shepherd in a dry paddock watching over his flock of long-tailed sheep.

They were on the flat, but with three kilometres still to go, it was clear they would soon be climbing into nearby hills. If they followed the direct line indicated by the GPS they would be in steep, difficult terrain, so they chose a rough, clay cattle track that was approximate to the right direction, and pounded their way up the hill between fences of yellow-flowered cactus plants.

Another shepherd left his flock and followed them at a safe distance as they passed through his village's farmland. When the expedition stopped to catch its breath, he caught up and shook their hands before departing. El Líder was certain that pale-skinned explorers in shorts and sandals were not a common sight here.

A woman and some smiling children with a donkey gazed as they passed by. El Líder did not stop. He had no desire to explain what they were doing—even if communication had been possible.

Speed and intensity, he sensed, were the expedition's friends, so that by the time residents of one village were aware of their presence, they would already be in the next—leaving any objectors in their wake. To confound even further, expedition members never failed to wave and smile as they swept past.

They skirted scattered houses nestled into the hillside. They followed paths that were carved deep by years of foot traffic. They crossed the brow of a hill and dropped down into a fig tree orchard where two little girls were homeward bound with armloads of hay. El Líder waved and smiled and the girls smiled back.

Expedition members carefully dodged small plots of vegetables growing between the trees, and headed for the open spaces where cereal crops had been harvested recently.

Clear of all the houses, they stopped briefly at a well where frogs croaked in the cool depths. The temperature was rising though it was still within the realms of a lovely summer's day.

They climbed through a barbed wire fence, crossed a motorway, and followed another dirt path through a scattered village. A track took them past a farmhouse where some noisy dogs emerged and chased them until the owner called them back. El Líder looked over his shoulder but did not stop.

They strode across a soccer field with a surface entirely of dirt, and goalposts made from logs, then stumbled on into a forest of scrawny pines that gave way to a plantation of cork trees—their brick-red trunks stripped of their bark.

They had been walking solidly for a couple of hours, and now that there were trees as far as they could see in every direction, they paused. They did not know where they were and El Líder doubted that they could find their way back to where they had come from. Technically they were lost.

The two things they did have were plenty of water, and the GPS which told them that their goal was just a kilometre away. El Líder rather wished they had also packed a lunch.

The last half hour took them through a eucalypt forest into a beautiful valley of well-fenced farmland surrounded by low, forested hills. A narrow, bitumen road ran round one edge of the valley. A small bridge with white rails crossed a stream and large trees threw cool shadows across their path. It was an idyllic scene and El Líder was filled with anticipation of an antipodes with a perfectly idyllic 360-degree view.

They crossed the road and climbed a fence into a field of wheat stubble. With just a few hundred metres to go, El Líder would gladly have asked permission to enter but there was no one to ask.

He led the way through the field, past a large derelict villa, then up a gentle slope towards the far side of the valley.

He was beginning to worry that the antipodes of his first Perfect Place would be in the forest, but at a small rocky outcrop just short of the trees, the GPS indicated that they had arrived.

They stopped and looked around. In a valley with so many scenic picture opportunities, the antipodes of BRIDGE, KERIKERI was a most ordinary place, but El Líder reminded himself that however it looked, it was *the* place, *the* antipodes of the bridge at Kerikeri he had stood on six months earlier. Beneath their feet, more than 12,000 kilometres away, vertically, was an upside-down bridge crossing an upside-down stream in the upside-down land of New Zealand.

There was no time for further reflection. The sooner they had the photos, the less chance of being prevented from getting them by an irate farmer.

Antipodes of bridge, Kerikeri.

As a centrepiece, El Líder could find nothing better than a white flower with an intricate geometric pattern that reminded him of the ancient Moorish mosaic art of *zellige* he had seen on the internet. Five minutes, and it was done.

That night, after the excitement of the expedition's ramble through the Moroccan countryside, El Líder sat on his Larache rooftop in the fading light enjoying a mild case of self-satisfaction.

The pressure to visit such tourist destinations as Marrakesh and Fez had been immense but he had followed the advice of Ralph Waldo Emerson and gone '… where there is no path…', to an empty field in an unknown corner of the world, and had found the antipodes of the BRIDGE, KERIKERI.

It was not much, but it was a start.

They were soon on their way again—leaving Larache at high speed—north to Asilah. The driver of the *grand taxi* chopped through the gears and braked furiously, aiming to complete the trip more quickly than any other vehicle that day.

The road was sealed but narrow. For more than an hour, the driver's yellow Merc swerved in and out between trucks, tractors, and donkey carts. El Líder wanted to tell him that speed was not the most important thing to the expedition but instead sat tense and sweating in the front passenger's seat. He counted five near-death experiences as they overtook lines of vehicles then, seemingly, became trapped on the wrong side of the road in the face of oncoming traffic. But each time the slimmest of gaps opened up and the old Merc lurched back to safety.

Alive but shaken, the explorers were an easy mark for touts as, tourist-like, they weaved their way in a daze through Asilah's streets in search of accommodation.

Within minutes they had been milked of a large number of

dirham by the friendly man who insisted on helping them find a small tourist hotel with low-budget rooms and high-budget prices.

El Líder was determined, thereafter, not to like Asilah. It was cleaner and tidier than Larache—its medina a maze of neat, narrow, whitewashed alleys with doors and other detail an appealing cobalt blue. But he was suspicious that the paint scheme was chosen merely to please the tourists. Certainly there was a great deal of painting going on and new buildings going up.

Other expedition members were happy being tourists for a while, and shopped for trinkets to take home. A genuine fake Rolex was almost bought but its clasp was broken, and a ceramic salad bowl in the *zellige* style at 'Little Ali's' shop was inspected closely but passed up in case of a better bargain around the corner.

Walk, talk, eat and drink seemed to be the main pursuits of Asilah locals, and the expedition fell into step, ordering fresh fish and couscous at a street-side café. La Campaña looked suspiciously at her tall glass of hot water and sugar, crammed full of sprigs of fresh mint. She took just the one sip of Morocco's famous mint tea.

A large man rode by on a small donkey and an old horse stumbled by pulling a cartload of cement bags. A poorly-dressed, unhappy-looking man wandered the streets, trying to sell beach umbrellas; another offered finely woven robes, another peanuts, another single cigarettes.

After a hot, prickly night on a damp mattress, El Líder vowed that they would leave Asilah just as soon as the sun came up. The call to prayer came; the cocks crowed; La Campaña swatted mosquitoes. 'Oh, they're so slow!' she exclaimed with delight, standing on the bed, her sandal poised over her head.

The white town with blue doors glowed in the early morning light, the air was warm and humid, and the sky a clear, light blue. But they packed up and left anyway.

The explorers spent most of the day on a bus heading for the sacred Islamic mountain fortress town of Chefchaouen. El Líder was delighted that on the way, at a point about 50 kilometres inland from the famous Moroccan port of Tangier, they passed within six kilometres of his next goal: the antipodes of MUNICIPAL CHAMBERS, WHANGAREI.

He had planned that on the return trip, he would vacate the bus at this nearest point and walk to the antipodes, while the rest of the expedition would continue on to Tangier and wait for him at the ferry terminal there.

Meanwhile, the bus carried them through a sinister landscape of quarries and scattered industrial complexes, of valleys filled with a foul-smelling blue smoke from a huge rubbish fire high on a hill, and of dry fields strewn with millions of partly-inflated supermarket shopping bags.

El Líder began to question the wisdom of asking to be left, alone, on the side of the road in this landscape. But he could think of no alternative.

After a good night's sleep in a Chefchaouen pension, the explorers loaded their packs on their backs again and set out for the bus station and the return trip to Tangier.

El Líder had not much enjoyed the bus ride to Chefchaouen, so found himself an easy target for the smooth-talking *grand taxi* drivers lurking near the bus station. He soon settled on a price for a taxi ride all the way to the ferry at Tangier, and the expedition loaded their packs into the boot.

El Líder explained to the driver that at a particular point along the way he would need to stop the taxi and wait — probably for two hours.

'No problem. No problem. This is your car. You say "Stop" and I will stop. No problem, no problem.' The driver smiled cheerfully. 'You can go where you like. You just have to say.'

El Líder had no idea how long it would actually take him to

complete a 12-kilometre round trip on foot but he felt certain it would not be less than two hours.

On the way down the sunny mountain slopes, they passed shepherds watching flocks of sheep and goats graze stony river flats, and farmers leading strong little donkeys piled high with straw collected from the fields.

The old Merc's radio broadcast in French. La Campaña heard a weather forecast and picked out the words for 'thirty-seven degrees'.

With one eye El Líder watched the GPS, and with the other he noted the increasing prevalence of big, iron-clad buildings, electricity pylons, substations and dusty, dirt roads full of trucks.

After two hours—on a deserted stretch of road 5.6 kilometres from the antipodes of Whangarei—El Líder suddenly called out, 'Stop!'

The driver hesitated but El Líder was firm. The taxi pulled into the gravel.

'Two hours,' he said to the driver as he reached for his backpack.

The driver frowned, deeply perplexed.

'Deux heures? What you do? You go to ferry!'

El Líder was patient.

'Yes, but as I explained before we started, I want to stop here for two hours first.'

'Nooooo,' said the driver in shock and disbelief.

'Two hours,' said El Líder making to get out of the taxi.

'No. You must not. For your own safety,' the driver pleaded. 'This is not Chefchaouen. The people here are dangerous.'

El Líder paused. This was valuable local knowledge to add to the misgivings he already had.

'They will point a gun at your head and steal all you have,' said the driver, his eyes wide with concern.

Half in, half out of the taxi, El Líder wavered; began

considering his options; began considering the possibility that a photograph from the taxi window of the point 5.6 kilometres from the antipodes of Whangarei might be all he needed.

But La Campaña was brisk. 'Just give me the passports and the money,' she said to El Líder as if that was some sort of solution to the problem.

El Líder was not certain he had yet given the matter enough thought, but stepped out of the taxi and handed passports, travellers cheques, credit card and cash through the window to La Campaña. She handed him his backpack, a small water bottle, and the two bananas left over from the previous night's tea.

The driver made it clear that although he was concerned about El Líder he was not so concerned that he would wait two hours. He gave El Líder two litres of water and shook his hand solemnly.

El Líder had included scraps of internet information about the Moroccan countryside in the expedition bible and one referred to the fierce Berber nomads. A hundred years ago, the land beyond the coastal cities was known as the Land of Lawlessness, and the Moroccan correspondent for *The Times* once wrote: 'The whole life in those great Atlas fortified kasbahs was one of warfare and of gloom. Every tribe had its enemies, every family its blood-feuds and every man his would-be murderer.'

The taxi sped off towards Tangier, and El Líder was alone. He turned to look in the direction the GPS indicated he should go. A dry, rocky hill stretched from the road to the sky—the top perhaps two kilometres away.

He set off into the landscape as fast as he could go—hoping that the further he got from the road, the less likely he would be to meet anyone. His eyes scanned the hillside ahead while his ears were pricked for the sound of raised voices from behind. He heard nothing and did not look back.

A few shrubs grew in some gullies but mostly he was climbing an expanse of dry, open grassland interspersed with rocky outcrops and patches where crops had been recently harvested.

He spotted a shepherd tending his sheep and he slunk by, doubled over, without being seen, and strode on rapidly—not fazed by the heat and the increasing steepness.

At the top of the hill—with four kilometres to go—he found himself on the edge of a quarry. He could hear diesel engines working hard. He moved to the left around the massive hole, aware he was on the skyline and easily visible. He slowed down a little, fancying that if he adopted the right walk and attitude, then from a distance he might be mistaken—in his white business shirt and long shorts and sandals—for a geologist or, if not a geologist, then at least someone entitled to be there.

He came across a quarry road and, as he made to cross it, a dump truck rounded the corner. El Líder was caught in the open and, expecting trouble, cursed his impatience.

The teenager at the wheel gave him a wave and shouted, '*Ola,*' with a big, white smile. El Líder waved back and smiled with relief, and the truck ground on up the hill.

He followed narrow, dusty paths down the hill through small fields lined with cactus plants and decrepit picket fences.

An old woman at a well looked up wide-eyed as he passed through a village otherwise deserted in the midday heat. Two mad dogs barked at him but did not approach.

He crossed the floor of the valley and then paused briefly to drink a litre of water before making his way up a hill even more barren than the first. Two farmers herding goats in the distance stopped and watched as he slid across slopes of loose rock and dropped down into another dry stream bed.

He was heading for another quarry—much bigger this time. The steep slopes around the edge of the crater were covered in greenery and from a distance looked cool and inviting. El Líder hoped the GPS would take him in that direction.

He had been going an hour and a half and, though pleased at his speed, he was disappointed that many small detours meant slow progress towards the antipodes.

He reached the edge of the quarry and peered down cautiously at the machinery working far below. He saw some figures in orange and white and ducked his head so as not to be seen, then surveyed the thin strip of cleared ground around the edge of the crater. It looked dangerous so he set off down a goat track leading away from the crater and into the dense, head-high bush.

When the track ran out, he retraced his steps and found another but it ran out, too, and he was forced to use his shoulder to barge his way through. A large, fat spider with a strong web clung to him and made him shiver.

He climbed large boulders that took him out of the bush onto small, smooth islands surrounded by a green sea, but every time, he was forced to drop back in again.

After more than an hour and less than a kilometre, he finally burst out of the bush into a pleasant valley of cork trees recently stripped of their bark. He found a track and sped off down the hill in high spirits. He was so close now. Just 600 metres away.

He avoided the worst of the bush until 50 metres from the antipodes where he was left with no choice but to worm his way back in, to the point where the GPS said he had arrived. He was in a clearing about a metre square, standing on a small pile of uninteresting rocks. All around him was a wall of shrubs with small green leaves and spindly, brittle branches. In the distance were some hills and the edge of a quarry.

The antipodes of MUNICIPAL CHAMBERS, WHANGA-REI, was neither a pole nor a peak. It was a very ordinary place with unspectacular views. But El Líder felt that it was a damn fine place for an explorer of slender abilities.

His legs and arms were scratched; one ankle was gouged and

Antipodes of Municipal Chambers, Whangarei.

bleeding and the other was sprained or strained. His shorts were torn and he was dripping with sweat.

But, oh, what an exhilarating cross-country march it had been. For a few intoxicating hours he was beyond the crowded confines of the public domain and away from the narrow corridors of traffic-filled highways.

He had no doubt trespassed many times but he had done no harm and he felt no remorse. He was harmless and remorseless. El Líder the nomad. El Líder the scout ant with a licence to roam.

On the verge of over-confidence, he decided not to retrace his steps to the point where the taxi had left him. He had glimpsed Tangier at one point and felt he could rely on his in-built sense of direction to guide him back to the highway he had started from, but via a different route. He had no map and his GPS would be of no help now.

Resting in a field of wheat straw and stubble, he ate his bananas and looked down on a peaceful valley with scattered farmhouses but no sign of life.

Of the four litres of water he had started with, he had just one left, and now his sips were short and cautious. He set off around the side of a hill, stumbling on loose earth and rocks as he sought a way through a cactus hedge.

High above, he could see a whitewashed villa and two women in robes and headscarves standing outside, watching him silently. A third figure was heading down the hill to intercept him. El Líder could see no weapon.

As their paths converged, El Líder could tell the figure was that of a boy of about 12. They stopped and looked at each other — El Líder dusty, red-faced and sweating; the boy cool, dark-skinned, with shining black eyes.

The boy offered his hand, bowed slightly and smiled. El Líder did likewise. They did not speak but as he continued on towards Tangier, El Líder began to feel as safe here amongst these farming families as he would in the Whangarei countryside.

Bolder now, he entered a small village where another young man was hauling a bucket of water up from a well. With a gentle sweep of his arm, the young man invited him to sit in the shade beside the well, next to a cool, stone horse trough.

Two smiling women in bare feet and vivid black and gold robes stopped nearby and called out greetings and questions in Arabic and French. El Líder replied in English but they did not respond.

He downed the last of his water and held out his empty bottle but the young man seemed reluctant to take it.

One of the women called out, '*Mal*!' El Líder understood, withdrew his hand and called out his thanks. He set off again with his backpack full of empty water bottles.

A fiercely strong tailwind helped him climb towards a pass where he found a tap and another horse trough but no water. The hills around him were barren and empty but he was reassured by glimpses of Tangier and the Straits of Gibraltar on the horizon.

It was mid afternoon, and with a long way to walk and nothing much else to think about, he recalled how close he had come to having breakfast. On the way to the taxi depot, the expedition had stopped at a small bread shop where La Campaña had inspected a stack of loaves closely and declared them not fresh enough. He thought about those loaves and he also thought about water. Quite a lot.

Eventually, just a kilometre from the highway, he came to a farmhouse where an elderly Arab woman filled his bottle with cool, clear water. A dozen excited junior members of her family tumbled out of the doorway to take a look at him, and waved cheerfully as he left. It was a most hospitable end to a trek through the Land of Lawlessness.

A bus and a taxi got him to Tangier's ferry terminal where his first priority was to enjoy a final glass of Morocco's fresh, sweet, orange juice before he crossed the straits to Spain.

El Líder's search of the internet for connections between New Zealand and Morocco had found that oranges were one.

Frances Hodgkins's 1905 painting, 'The Orange Sellers' featured Tangier which suggested to El Líder she, too, had probably enjoyed the juice. He emptied his glass and went off to meet up with the rest of the expedition.

9

ANTIPODES OF AUCKLAND

The expedition's trip from New Zealand to the antipodes—around the circumference of the earth—had been 20,038 kilometres. Travelling direct, on the other hand, would have been much shorter—about 12,752 kilometres, depending on which part of the earth was measured.

The direct route required 30 kilometres of digging to get through the earth's crust followed by the 720 kilometres of the upper mantle, the 2,171 kilometres of the lower mantle, the 2,259 kilometres of the outer core and the 1,221 kilometres of the inner core. And at that point the digger would be only halfway and suffering considerably from the heat.

El Líder had typed 'hole through the centre of the earth' into Google and was astounded to find 40 million sites. He ignored all but the one that explained how many minutes it would take for someone who jumped into such a hole to travel from New Zealand to the antipodes. The answer was 42.

It did not escape his attention that 42 was also the answer to life, the universe, and everything, but he could not work out whether or not this was just a coincidence.

The expedition hired a Ford Focus diesel station wagon in Spain and drove to Gibraltar to get their bearings before heading off into the Iberian Peninsula.

El Líder had overlooked the fact that as well as Morocco, Spain and Portugal, Gibraltar would have antipodes in New Zealand,

and he was disappointed not to have a Perfect Place antipodes to find there. Expedition members, however, seemed not to mind, and turned their attention to doing laundry, writing postcards and reading English language newspapers over 'the full English breakfast'.

Their first goal in Spain was the antipodes of TAKAPUNA BEACH, AUCKLAND which required them to head north from the Mediterranean coast and climb into the Serrania de Ronda — the rugged, mountain region in Andalucía where 'white villages' were clustered on hilltops like sun-baked barnacles. Internet sites described it as a wild and romantic landscape where once *bandoleros* had their dens and attacked travellers on lonely mountain passes.

The expedition was alone on the smooth, winding mountain road and the only hold-ups were caused by road crews building neat rock walls to stop tourists, distracted by the scenery, from tumbling into dry ravines.

La Campaña took charge of the GPS as the barren hills gave way to rolling fields of sunflowers and grapevines. The temperature was in the low 40s, but the Focus's air-conditioning worked superbly.

They drove around the clifftop town of Ronda — the home of Spanish bullfighting — and a forested valley brought them to within 300 metres of the antipodes of Takapuna Beach.

El Líder pulled off the road, climbed out of the Focus, and looked up at the sides of the valley. The 300 metres appeared almost vertical and the face was covered in dense, mature forest. Impenetrable, he thought.

But there was a bigger problem. On the other side of the high, rusty, barbed-wire fence nearby were two animals lurking in the shadows.

'El Toro,' El Líder murmured under his breath.

He took a careful look at the fence and another look at the

cattle with their magnificently broad, curved horns. They might look placid, but who knew what else was hiding in the shadows? He hesitated.

'Don't be a wuss,' said La Campaña loudly.

El Líder remembered for a moment an old man from Penrith he had heard about, who died on the horns of his prized bull.

La Campaña could say what she liked, he decided, and climbed back into the Focus. They drove on, hoping to circle the antipodes of Takapuna and consider it from another angle.

They got to within 1.3 kilometres by taking a narrow, sealed country road through the Parque Natural Sierra de Grazalema. The distance would be no great obstacle but the wire fences looked as if they would be. It was too late in the day and too hard and too hot to strategise so they booked into the nearby country hotel, Hotel de Campo.

The owner explained that the cattle would have been cows of a special lean-beef variety and quite harmless provided their calves were not interfered with.

They rested for an hour or two then at sunset, as the day cooled, La Campaña and El Líder set out on foot for the antipodes.

There was no track to follow and they were forced to make their own way through a forest of cork trees — dodging thistles and spider webs as they went. They startled a deer and watched it swim through a farmer's cereal crop.

Eventually, with five kilometres still to go, their half-hearted attempt petered out next to a high fence of tight netting and barbed wire and they decided, instead, to drive into the home of bullfighting for dinner and a walk around its clifftop walls. How unfortunate, thought El Líder, that the antipodes of Takapuna Beach was not in Ronda itself where there were picturesque vantage points at every turn.

Ronda, his expedition bible noted, claimed to have Spain's oldest, biggest, and most beautiful bullring — the Plaza de

Toros—and the legendary Pedro Romero killed over 5,000 bulls there in the 18th century—the last one when he was 79 years old. Other sources suggested that Ronda's bullring was not the biggest but might be the widest and was certainly one of the most elegant.

It was not an argument El Líder wanted to get involved in and, because it was not the antipodes of a Perfect Place, he was content with a quick look at a bronze statue of 'El Toro' standing outside the bullring, before joining the expedition on a search for some typical Spanish cuisine. They found excellent pizza and beer at a picturesque tourist café.

In the morning La Campaña opted for a pre-breakfast swim while El Líder, in shorts and sandals, headed back into the hills. He counted four different varieties of thistle in the first 200 metres and there was gorse, too, although it was weak and spindly. The fences had a top strand of rusty barbed wire at eye level, another at chin level and a third at throat level. The barbs were less than a handspan apart and the holes in the wire netting were too small for the toes of his sandals. The first fence-climb, into a field of goats and cork trees, cost him torn shorts and a torn arm.

He climbed another fence into a crop of what looked like wild oats and, determined to do no damage, walked around the edge through tall, spindly weeds including a fifth variety of thistle.

As he came over the crest of a hill, he found he was in a barren paddock with about 100 large, dark-grey pigs that were feeding along the far fenceline. He wheeled away rapidly before they saw him, and headed for the nearest fence which was a very long way off. He began sizing up each cork tree he passed for climbability.

The pigs had seemed peaceful enough but he had already encountered the remains of a pig he imagined had been cannibalized, and Spanish pigs owed him no favours. He had requested *jamón* for lunch the previous day and had enjoyed the thin, salty slices.

As he rounded a rock, he almost ran into two pigs. They stopped eating and looked up. El Líder veered off again, moving rapidly downhill, glancing over his shoulder. The pigs watched him suspiciously.

He scrambled over fence after fence until he felt certain he was pig-free.

Finally, 150 metres from his goal, he came across a splendid view of Ronda set in a groomed countryside of gold and green.

The potential for a very pretty antipodes to Takapuna Beach raised El Líder's spirits and he charged down through the cork tree forest into a little valley.

He stopped and looked around, checking the GPS to make sure he had not made a mistake.

He was in a clearing. At his feet were a few clumps of dried grass in the dust. There was a spindly shrub crawling with ants.

He could see Ronda in the distance but it was partly obscured by a rusty, metal power pole. Another ugly pole spoiled the view in the opposite direction There were power lines overhead and there were scattered thistles and gorse.

El Líder refused to be disappointed, and snapped a roll of film, but he could not shake off the feeling that a different North Shore Perfect Place would have landed him in much more elegant Spanish surroundings.

It began to rain as he rushed into the splendid hotel dining room to join the other explorers for breakfast and unlimited fresh orange juice, unsweetened muesli, and croissants with cheese and *jamón*.

Antipodes of Takapuna Beach.

Half an hour in the Focus brought them to the archaeological site of Acinipo at the end of a narrow road about 20 kilometres from Ronda.

El Líder was looking for the antipodes of BAYSWATER MARINA, ACROSS THE HARBOUR FROM AUCKLAND CITY.

The expedition bible described Acinipo as a first-century Roman hilltop town which once had a population of 5000, an array of public buildings, a theatre seating 2000, and its own coins featuring bunches of grapes. It disappeared when the empire fell.

From the car park, El Líder could see nothing more than a few heaps of stones and a man in a booth waiting to take his money, he presumed. As with Lixus, this was an ancient ruin of peripheral interest. El Líder was far more interested in the dry farm nearby.

While the other expedition members waited in the Focus, he walked up a long gravel driveway to a farmhouse to ask permission to proceed. He could see an elderly man standing outside the house with a hairy chihuahua at his feet, and was delighted at the prospect of being able to speak to a genuine Auckland antipodean.

The dog saw El Líder approaching and ran down the driveway to meet him. Though small, it had an extraordinarily loud bark and as El Líder walked towards the man, the dog circled him and barked loudly.

'*Ola*!' shouted El Líder when he reached the man.

'*Ola*,' said the man, oblivious to the dog which continued to circle and bark.

El Líder had prepared a suitable sentence in Spanish for just such an occasion and had even written it down on a piece of paper in Spanish, French, Portuguese, German, and Arabic so that if his pronunciation failed he could hand over the written version.

It went something like this: 'I am from New Zealand on the other side of the world and I would like to take a photograph at the antipodes which happens to be on your land.'

Unfortunately, he had left the written version in the car by mistake and, although he could remember some of it, he was finding it difficult to concentrate. He felt certain that if he let the dog out of his sight as it circled behind him, it would dart in and nip him on the ankle. Rabies.

He reverted to pidgin English and sign language—pointing at his camera and at the antipodes on the hill nearby where he wished to take his photos.

The elderly man was very friendly and spoke at length in Spanish. El Líder listened thoughtfully while watching the circling dog out the corner of his eye. He began to get the impression that the man was suggesting that there were many better places for photos than the middle of the dreary field next to his house, but El Líder pointed again and smiled and would have none of it.

When the man finished speaking, El Líder thanked him and walked off down the driveway—careful not to accidentally step on the paw of the little dog and send it scurrying off into the shrubbery. It barked him off the property and then turned and minced away up the driveway.

La Campaña and El Líder walked a short distance down the road towards the antipodes.

As they began wading into the field through waist-high weeds and thistles, a car drew up and a man jumped out and began a conversation with La Campaña.

El Líder thought he could hear French being spoken and after a time came to the conclusion that the man wanted to know how far it was to the end of the road and the ancient ruin of Acinipo.

'*Deux kilometre,*' said El Líder helpfully, pointing to make sure the man and his passengers understood.

The conversation continued and El Líder then deduced that

Antipodes of Bayswater Marina.

the man wanted to know if there was a restaurant at the end of the road. 'No, no,' he interrupted again, with a heavy foreign accent, to assist La Campaña as she attempted to answer the man's stream of questions.

The conversation resumed then the man thanked La Campaña, climbed into his car and, with a look of relief, drove off.

La Campaña explained to El Líder that the conversation had been in Spanish, that the man was looking for a petrol station, and that he had no interest in restaurants or where the road ended. El Líder's confidence was momentarily shaken.

They continued walking across a high hill. Although a few sunflowers brightened the scene, the antipodes of Bayswater was in a field containing some sort of dry, burnt, brown crop while, just 20 metres away was a superb view down a valley to a castle that was perched on the top of a small, conical hill and surrounded by neat rows of olive trees and fields of sunflowers and cereal.

El Líder was tempted to move his antipodes just a little, for a better view, but his conscience would not allow him. He might not be finding the best views in Spain, he told himself, but no one would ever be able to accuse him of being deliberately inaccurate.

La Campaña had suggested at one point that he include some photos of birds from the internet. 'Who would know?' she asked.

'I would,' El Líder said, in a superior way.

He took the photographs and they were soon on the trail of the antipodes of WATERFRONT SCULPTURE, AUCKLAND, just a few kilometres away.

The GPS led them up a narrow, dirt track to the edge of a cliff overlooking a broad expanse of golden countryside. They were in a yard with a wind-sock, a sign prohibiting entry, a rough building and a friendly black labrador. Although there was a car, no one was about, and El Líder stood on the breezy cliff-edge for several minutes and thought hard.

Four hundred metres below, in a field of gold, was the antipodes. He could clamber down the cliff face, which was steep and covered in dry scrub. He could walk carefully around the edges of the crops over the loose, stony soil. He could leave the rest of the expedition in the car in the baking, midday sun. He could, on his hands and knees perhaps, clamber back up the cliff. He would, no doubt, gather a few dozen more scars on his legs.

But he had never really taken to his WATERFRONT SCULPTURE, AUCKLAND Perfect Place, so the expedition climbed back into the Focus and headed away from this antipodes with the air-conditioning on full.

El Líder had the antipodes of three more Auckland Perfect Places to choose from, and followed the GPS into a farmyard where half a dozen dogs began to bark. He could see the antipodes for AUCKLAND TOWN HALL, QUEEN STREET, 600 metres away at the top of a hill.

There was no one home, but rather than waiting for the farmer to return so he could ask permission, he reached for his backpack and camera and set off, leaving the expedition members with instructions to show the farmer, if he returned, the carefully constructed sentence in five languages.

The first paddock was wheat stubble, which added more scratches to El Líder's bare legs.

He skirted a field of rapidly ripening sunflowers and began climbing a cultivated paddock of loose soil—lumps of earth getting between his feet and his sandals and adding to his discomfort.

He entered an olive grove, paused in the shade, and reached for the water bottle he now remembered leaving in the car.

As he scrambled up a steeper slope through dried thistles and bracken, he began to suspect he was about to encounter a problem and as he reached the top of a ridge, his suspicions were confirmed.

The antipodes of AUCKLAND TOWN HALL, QUEEN STREET was 149 metres into a sea of golden wheat.

El Líder stopped to look and think. He could easily wade to the antipodes without being seen from below. But he was already nervous about his lack of permission and, besides, one of the expedition's rules was that it would do no harm.

The simple solution was to ignore the rule or even to pretend that the rule never existed. No one would ever know. Choices and consequences swirled around him confusingly. The sun beat down. He was hot, thirsty, and frustrated.

Sir Edmund, he knew, had not hesitated on Everest: 'I looked up to the right and there was a rounded snowy dome. It must be the summit! We drew closer together as Tenzing brought in the slack on the rope. I continued cutting a line of steps upwards. Next moment I had moved onto a flattish exposed area of snow with nothing but space in every direction. Tenzing quickly joined me and we looked around in wonder.'

But this was not virgin snow at the top of the world. It was wheat, or maybe barley; El Líder was never sure.

Time passed. Finally, with a sigh, he turned his back on the crop and from where he stood 149 metres from the antipodes of AUCKLAND TOWN HALL, he took photos of his best view yet, and scrambled back down to the Focus. He had been away two hours. Everything was as he left it: dogs barking and expedition members trying to sleep.

At the nearest intersection he had the choice of heading left for the mountain village of El Gastor — once the hideaway of one of the last bandits of the Serrania — José María "El Tempranillo" — or the tourist temptations of Ronda.

He chose Ronda and a tasty outdoor *tapas* lunch of prawns in batter, tuna mousse, smoky sausage, and white asparagus in cream sauce.

Antipodes of Auckland Town Hall, Queen Street.

El Líder had his long-awaited first encounter with anchovies during a La Campaña-led break from the expedition. She had insisted that they visit the Costa del Sol on the Mediterranean Sea—even though it was not the antipodes of any Perfect Place.

El Líder perked up, a little, when he found anchovies on the lunch menu at a bar in a deserted beach resort near Cadiz. A waitress brought him a large, deep-fried pile of fishes. He bent over the plate and waded in with a fork, pausing every so often to glance up and down the deserted beach and out towards the flat, grey sea.

The Spanish anchovies were bigger than the oily little slivers El Líder was used to eating from a can in New Zealand, and the bones were crunchy. He offered the other explorers a taste but they declined and he ate on, alone. It had been a generous serving, and when he came to the last anchovy, he hesitated. He appreciated now how an albatross would feel as it prepared to head home to feed its chick at the end of a week's fishing.

La Campaña believed that the bar's toilets were the cleanest she had found in Spain, and El Líder gave the Café Negra an eight.

They moved on to Jerez de la Frontera and acquired a temporary taste for sherry as they toured the Tio Pepe *bodega*.

El Líder was at his most attentive when their tour guide explained that Spanish explorer Magellan spent more on sherry for his round-the-world expedition than on guns and ammunition, and he also took note when told that sherry was best served at seven degrees Celsius in a tapered glass. But mostly his attention was left to drift aimlessly on the warm, sweet, dreamy air of the sherry cellars.

They left the shady *bodega*, stepped out onto a sun-beaten street clutching an expensive bottle of sherry '... with a beautiful mahogany colour ... an iodine-tinged upper layer and a very elegant leg ...' and, still slightly lubricated by the sherry sampling,

El Líder climbed into the Focus and steered it back into the Spanish traffic. He cruised through roundabouts like a native, and slipped in and out of small spaces as if born to it. Gone was the nervousness and hesitation of driving on the wrong side of the road and steering from the wrong side of the car.

Alcohol and driving might not mix in New Zealand but on the opposite side of the world a little sherry before driving was having an excellent effect. They sped towards Sevilla to drop a departing explorer at the airport.

The detour provided El Líder with the chance to visit Sevilla Cathedral—considered to be the world's largest gothic structure—and in particular the tomb of the world's most famous explorer, 'The Illustrious and Prominent Varon Don Cristobal Colón'.

Some of Colón's bones were said to lie in a great lead casket inside the cathedral which the explorers found to be a very cool place in which to get out of the midday sun.

There was no explanation of why Colón's name was changed to Christopher Columbus at some point, and on consulting the internet later, El Líder wished he had never asked. At least one internet scholar was offering millions of words on the subject.

But for a New Zealand explorer, such as himself, it was intriguing to discover that some of the bones of the famous explorer who sailed the ocean blue in 1492 were buried at the antipodes of somewhere off the coast of Raglan. Other expedition members were not so impressed and they soon headed off through the narrow streets of Sevilla in search of a good cup of coffee and a seat in the shade.

Next morning, as they packed the Focus, La Campaña was in a highly good mood, having won an argument with the Hotel San Pablo's receptionist who had dared suggest charging extra for the hotel's basement car park.

'I don't think so!' said La Campaña with great finality as the Focus swept out of the park and into the quiet, early-morning streets of Sevilla.

The next stop would be the antipodes of BETWEEN THE FLAGS, PIHA BEACH—a point not too far from Sevilla but, more accurately, quite near the farming town of Montellano (pop. 7,000).

It took an hour to get to Montellano which seemed to be an exceptionally wealthy village of narrow, tidy streets and rows of neat two-storey villas with polished wooden doors and ornate vertical steel bars across their front windows.

El Líder could find out almost nothing about the town in advance except for its one brush with fame when Francisco Goya, considered to be 'the father of modern art', painted a highwayman there.

The GPS directed the explorers not to stop until they reached a small bridge a few kilometres beyond the village and 3.27 kilometres from their goal. This did not seem like a great distance as they contemplated it in the cool interior of the Focus.

They began by walking up a dusty farm track towards an olive grove, El Líder with three litres of water in his backpack but no food, expecting to be back in time for lunch.

They were soon in a recently harvested wheat field with the sort of straw El Líder could imagine a small man with a long beard spinning into gold.

He also imagined, as they climbed the empty fields towards the skyline, that there would be a shady olive tree at the top where they could rest and enjoy the view. But at the top there was neither a small man nor a shady tree. Stretching out ahead was a patchwork of rolling fields all the way to the misty horizon. El Líder was not sure what made the horizon misty but he was certain it was not water vapour.

Their path took them towards a huge field of sunflowers, and the expedition rule never to walk through crops was again brought into question, surrounded as they were on three sides. A detour around the edge of the crop would take them away from the Piha antipodes and, not only that, the detour was uphill while the direct route was downhill. And loose soil with large lumps made walking difficult.

Breathing hard, El Líder set out. They had been walking for an hour. His main complaint was about the scratches from the wheat stubble he was getting on his sandal-clad feet.

La Campaña had had the foresight to wear socks in her sandals and was spared the worst of the scratching. El Líder reminded her, though, that she had not had the good sense to wear more than a skimpy white top which did nothing to keep the sun from her shoulders, while he was at least sensibly dressed in his white, long-sleeved Hallensteins business shirt.

Eventually they found an area where the sunflowers were growing more sparsely, and by weaving carefully between the heavy seed-heads they slipped through without doing any damage.

In the distance they could see a herd of animals. El Líder's first thought was El Toro, though it was difficult to make out what sort of animals they were. As a precaution, they followed the edge of a very deep but empty ditch—a place El Líder was quite prepared to leap into at the least provocation.

It gradually became clear that the animals were horses standing quietly on a grassy knoll. La Campaña suggested that they ignore them and follow a direct line straight across the paddock, under their noses. El Líder made excuses and took the long way round, keeping to a wire fence he intended leaping over in the event of a stampede.

He did not like horses, having, as a child, been chased and bitten by the bad-tempered family pony, although the more he thought about it, the more he suspected that it might have been his brother who was chased. Either way, he was not about to trust these great, shiny Spanish stallions. Or mares.

The horses paid them no attention. Not even their ears pricked up and the expedition passed by untrampled.

There was no doubt about the next paddock. It was full of cattle—magnificent black beasts with wide-set horns. The GPS was determined to steer them into their midst.

They stopped 200 metres from their goal. The antipodes was on a hillside amongst some shady trees and in the shade of each tree were the cattle—black animals in dark shadows. El Líder could not tell if any bulls were present. He urged caution and carefully and quietly edged around an olive tree, watching for reaction from the cattle. La Campaña's approach was to assume she owned the place and march straight towards them.

Suddenly, the shadows were alive with noise and movement: El Toro was on the run—or at least the mothers of El Toro were keen to get out of La Campaña's way.

A few were reluctant to give up their places in the shade and trotted away just a few metres, presenting, El Líder was relieved to notice, haughty backsides rather than horns on lowered heads.

El Líder found the antipodes of BETWEEN THE FLAGS, PIHA BEACH and waited for the cattle to settle down so he could include them in his photographs. But they never really did and the pictures he got showed furtive cows searching for shady places. La Campaña, oblivious to their anxiety, sat in their preferred shady places and engaged in mortal combat with biting flies and annoying midges—or 'thunderflies', as she called them.

Barely pausing for breath, the explorers began to retrace their steps to the Focus and, as the sun climbed in the sky, struggled back up hills of stubble, crossed fences, and skirted sunflowers.

They were reduced at times to walking in short, rapid

Antipodes of between the flags, Piha Beach, Auckland.

bursts — pausing beneath each shady tree for a few minutes to gulp down mouthfuls of water.

At the top of a hill, El Líder lay in the coolness of an olive tree's shade and gazed out at the golden hills around them. The words of Sting that he had struggled to keep at bay during earlier encounters with Spain's wide open spaces once again swirled around inside his head — the ones about the west wind and the fields of barley.

The first verse came readily to him, but there was no time for more, even if he could have remembered the words; La Campaña was anxious to move on.

They passed the horses and the derelict stone barn and the olive groves again, and were forced to take a wide detour around some beehives they had not seen the first time.

Finally, they were back at the Focus. El Líder started the motor then lay down on the road in the shade of a eucalyptus tree while he waited for the air-conditioning to cool the car's interior.

It had taken them four hours and they were both exhausted. The television weather presenter that night would reveal the day's maximum temperature to have been 40 degrees Celsius.

El Líder decided that another principle of the expedition from this point onwards would be that three kilometres would be the maximum walking distance to any antipodes.

They drove to a bar in Montellino and downed lemonade and San Miguel, El Líder's adopted preferred beer, and tried to explain to the publican what they were doing.

He did not seem to understand the word 'antipodes' and El Líder suspected he had never heard of New Zealand, but he gave them tasty baked chillies, and potatoes in tomato, and little pieces of bread.

El Líder's enthusiasm for the food led the publican to proudly present him with the specialty of the house: a tall glass of chunky tomato and chilli sauce. With ice. El Líder managed a couple of sips but could not drink it, and La Campaña rejected his whispered pleas for help. They were left with no choice but to make an embarrassed exit—the offending glass left glowing on the bar.

Afterwards, while reading the expedition bible, El Líder discovered that Montellino was famous for not only tomato soup but also fish stew in white sauce and offal pudding. It could have been worse.

Antipodes of Government Gardens, Rotorua.

10
ANTIPODES OF
WELLINGTON NORTH

In contrast to Piha, GOVERNMENT GARDENS, ROTORUA was too easy. The explorers had spent the night in a town called Bailen where the Spanish scored a famous victory over Napoleon's French forces in 1808 but which was in no other way remarkable as far as El Líder could tell.

In the morning they shopped at a small *supermercardo* and bought a bottle of red wine for less than a dollar just because they could, then took the Madrid-Córdoba highway for a short time before pulling off onto a narrow gravel farm road leading to an olive grove.

They enjoyed a breakfast of croissants, orange juice, cheese and some thinly sliced meat-from-the-pig called *lomo*. A few minutes' walk brought them to the antipodes, where there was nothing but olive trees in every direction. The sound of cicadas was deafening. One landed on the ground, giving El Líder a convenient centre-piece. And that was it. The antipodes of ROTORUA on film. All done. Nothing to report.

What followed was a magical drive through rolling hills and manicured farmland—red soil, golden straw, blue sky, olive-green olive trees. The air was still and the sun was bright. There were no fences or animals or people and the road, though narrow, was comfortably smooth.

La Mancha!

The expedition bible described La Mancha as Spain's largest plain—its name originating from an Arabian word meaning 'dry land'. It also went into rather too much detail about its famous Manchego sheep's cheeses—made only from the whole milk of the Manchega sheep, aged for at least 60 days, and imprinted with a distinctive zigzag pattern. And the cheese was famous for being mentioned in *Don Quixote*.

La Mancha, of course, was the domain of El Líder's favourite Spanish explorer. Their first actual encounter with the Don was a green sign that read, 'Ruta de Don Quixote' and soon after that they came across a large stone plinth featuring a black silhouette of the Don, his servant, and his horse. It was near Villanueva de San Carlos, at the bottom of a road leading to a towering, fairytale castle boldly outlined against the sky. This, according to the sign, was Sacro Convento y Castillo de Calatrava la Nueva and it was closed to tourists.

El Líder calculated that the castle would have its antipodes somewhere in the North Island. The expedition bible explained that it was constructed in the thirteenth century by the winners of the battle of Navas de Tolosa—the Calatravos horsemen. The losers, no doubt, did the heavy lifting.

The castle was not one of the expedition's goals and El Líder was content to merely pause at its gates for a moment to observe the silhouette and then drive on a few kilometres across a rough mountain road to its end, 1.26 kilometres from the antipodes of JETBOAT, HUKA FALLS, TAUPO.

La Campaña poured orange juice and El Líder ate *lomo* and dry bread as, through the Focus's windscreen, they studied a steep hillside covered in thick, rough scrub.

On the way through the La Mancha countryside, La Campaña had seen a snake wriggling across the road. El Líder had not seen it but had felt it going under the wheels and now, looking up at the hillside with its rocky outcrops and dark crevices, he again thought of snakes.

He knew they were afraid of humans and would wriggle away as they approached. But who was to say a snake might not make a mistake and forget to wriggle away? He also recalled an earlier battle with Moroccan scrub—on the way to the antipodes of Whangarei.

They climbed out of the car, loaded up the backpack with water, and set out across a stretch of wheat stubble towards the hill. After just a minute or two, they encountered a wire fence, the top of which was well above their heads, and this time there were six strands of barbed wire. Also, at intervals, there were empty guard towers. This was not a fence to be trifled with.

That quite suited El Líder, and the Focus was soon bouncing its way back down the hill towards the first available café in the village of Villanueva de San Carlos. There was no one in the village except for two fierce-looking matrons on a doorstep, so La Campaña decided they should forget the coffee and make another attempt on the Huka Falls antipodes, by a different route.

A battered four-wheel-drive came up behind them as they meandered along a narrow gravel road, circling the antipodes. El Líder pulled over politely and the two fierce-looking occupants sped past the explorers as if they were road-kill.

The four-wheel-drive drove through a large, metal gate but by the time El Líder reached the gate it was closed again. And locked. They could see a very grand farmhouse on a hill in the distance but there were no people in sight.

El Líder and La Campaña discussed their options. They could wait by the gate in the hope the fierce men would return and let them in. Or, they could leave. El Líder had been ready to leave from the first moment he had seen the bleak, snake-infested hillside. La Campaña took time to be convinced but even she, eventually, agreed that it was the end of the road for HUKA FALLS and the explorers, feeling slightly guilty at their failure, turned tail.

If only HUKA FALLS had been a few hundred metres to the right, El Líder mused, they would have been at an antipodes with views of the magnificent castle with the long Spanish name.

El Líder never really expected that their route would take them past windmills. It was too much to expect. So when he saw two windmills of the Don Quixote type on a hillside, he immediately abandoned the search for the antipodes of REFLECTING BALL OVERLOOKING THE SEA, NAPIER, and turned off towards the village of Puerto Lapice — the very one mentioned by Cervantes.

The windmills were plainly visible above the village but no-where could they find the road that would take them there. After half an hour of driving up narrow roads, and back down again, of stopping and starting and reversing, La Campaña suggested they ask someone for directions. But El Líder declared that he was content with the view they had of the windmills from the plain and that it would not be improved by getting closer. La Campaña had a perplexed look on her face as, without further explanation, El Líder took the road out of the village and resumed the search for antipodes.

They planned to spend the night at Miguel Esteban, which was about halfway between the Mediterranean coast and Madrid, and as they neared the small town, late in the afternoon, they ran into a thunderstorm, complete with torrential rain, and lightning that struck the vineyards all around them.

They stopped outside a building that looked as if it might be a hotel, and La Campaña dashed through the rain to the reception area.

She returned dripping wet to explain to El Líder that the rooms were clean and tidy and the rate was reasonable.

They took a room; however, once again, El Líder found the air-conditioning to be less than adequate; he did not like the look of the pillow on the bed that was effectively two pillows joined together end-to-end — the bed's occupants expected to share — and, as well, they had a view over an empty paddock and a petrol station.

So this was 'two star', El Líder thought to himself.

They settled themselves into the empty restaurant and, to simplify communications with the non-English-speaking waiter, El Líder pointed to the 'La Mancha special'.

A *grande* plate arrived, covered in nothing but cold, sliced pig meat, and La Campaña, being vegetarian, left El Líder to cope on his own. The first *copa de vino* was fine, and the second even better.

The plains around Miguel Esteban were covered with grapevines — each vine sprawling across the ground, unsupported by posts and wires.

The vineyards contained a maze of narrow gravel roads and it was simply a matter of driving through the vineyards to get to the antipodes of REFLECTING BALL OVERLOOKING THE SEA, NAPIER.

El Líder was left with a mere 60 metres to walk, and every step took him closer to an old farm building rustically framed by a couple of trees and surrounded by vines. He took the photographs, using a bunch of green grapes for a centrepiece.

'Probably Tempranillo,' said La Campaña.

Unfortunately, the antipodes of BRONZE SCULPTURE, CENTRAL HASTINGS was in almost identical surroundings — lacking only the picturesque old farm building.

El Líder took the photographs anyway and returned to the Focus.

Antipodes of reflecting ball overlooking the sea, Napier.

Antipodes of bronze sculpture, Hastings.

They drove off towards the antipodes of JUST OUTSIDE THE CAVES, WAITOMO, which brought them to the outskirts of the village of Valmojado—internetly famous for its pyrotechnics and in particular its 'fire bulls' though what exactly a 'fire bull' might be El Líder never discovered.

The explorers had two kilometres to go to the Waitomo antipodes, and set out along a narrow footpath through dried grass and scrubby trees.

The footpath ran parallel to a high fence made of two layers of netting and numerous strands of barbed wire. The top of each post had three or four long, slender spikes that would prevent anyone from climbing them. And it soon became clear that the antipodes they were heading for was on the other side of this fence.

La Campaña examined places where some sort of animal had been able to squeeze under, but concluded, for the sake of her white top, that she would rather climb over.

In the vain hope that the fence would curve in the direction they wanted to go, they continued walking until, 1.3 kilometres from the antipodes, they came across a broken wire.

A decision was required: should they give up or bend the wire a little and crawl through the hole about half a metre from the ground? They had been walking for an hour and seen no one. And there were no animals.

In an instant they were through and rushing to the dark shadow of a nearby tree. They stopped and listened. Only the cicadas made any sound. El Líder recorded on his GPS where the broken wire was and they began walking to the antipodes of Waitomo through rolling fields of tall, dry grass.

El Líder noted some flattened patches where animals had been resting, and looked around for signs of El Toro but could see none. There were animal droppings but they were not bull. The landscape was very savannah-like. El Líder hoped for goats.

He was very conscious that they were trespassing and could not, as they had intended to do on previous occasions, plead ignorance. This time the fence and the signs could not be misunderstood.

With 400 metres to go, they came over a rise and there was the *casa*. They ducked behind a tree and peered out at the large building with whitewashed walls and a red-brown tiled roof. The GPS pointed them directly at it.

They retraced their steps, back to the bottom of a narrow valley where they were out of sight of the *casa*, and made off at right angles to the antipodes.

This time they encountered a road — the entrance to the *casa,* they suspected — but, worse, their way was blocked by a crop of some sort. There was no way through, and again they retraced their steps to the hidden valley. They set out again, intending to circle the *casa* in the opposite direction.

As they neared a cluster of trees, they were startled by a rustling sound ahead. They stopped and stared as a dozen deer with broad antlers stared back at them from the shadows.

A second later, the deer turned and crashed off towards the *casa* and the explorers ran off and huddled under a tree. They watched the *casa* through the branches and could see no movement there, but El Líder was losing his appetite for this antipodes. He was fairly certain the deer would stay ahead of them and continue to give the alarm, and he tried to visualise the conversation that would occur if they met the landowner. He did not like what he visualised.

They had only 600 metres to go but, on balance, El Líder decided the need for photographs of the antipodes of JUST OUTSIDE THE CAVES, WAITOMO was outweighed by the potential embarrassment of being caught, and he could see no way of approaching the property owners from where they were without having to explain how they got there. It was all too hard and the explorers suddenly fled.

La Campaña dived, head-first, through the hole in the fence

and bruised her thighs on the wire. El Líder followed, tearing his shorts again. They repaired the hole in the fence and ran off down the track, laughing like naughty children, and drove to a bar in Aldea El Fresno where La Campaña ordered a Campari for lunch—served large and straight with ice—and was soon, she said, 'sloshed'.

El Líder cleaned up a complimentary antipasta of stuffed eggs and pork crackling with his beer, then they swam in the river that ran through the town. Although the banks were littered with plastic, the water looked clean and clear, and the Kiwi explorers felt right at home as they dried off on the gravel and ate fresh bread and sun-melted cheese for lunch.

Not far off, they found the antipodes of WINDMILLS, PALMERSTON NORTH. It was a bus stop at the entrance to a safari park near Villa de Prado and it was only made interesting because it provided El Líder with his first opportunity to photograph an antipodean.

At the bus stop was a young man pacing up and down, deeply engrossed in a cellphone conversation. El Líder discreetly included him in photographs he was taking of the surrounding landscape—a dreary combination of tatty signs advertising the park, cars approaching and departing, and some vines over a fence.

La Campaña watched from the Focus, parked some distance up the road, as El Líder took photograph after photograph.

The young man put the cellphone away and told El Líder he worked at the park and was waiting to catch a bus home to Sevilla. He wandered off. El Líder continued to loiter and take photographs as the fancy took him—a passing truck here, a cigarette packet on the ground there, the young man in a better position.

Unbeknown to El Líder, La Campaña was becoming increasingly concerned about appearances. Standing in the surf at

Antipodes of windmills, Palmerston North.

Takapuna Beach taking photographs of other people's children in swimming costumes had been one thing, but taking surreptitious photographs of a young man at a bus stop was another.

There had been a brief, confused conversation with the young man at one point about whether El Líder might have a spare cigarette—which he did not, being a non smoker. And at another point it crossed El Líder's mind to offer the young man a lift. But before he could put the thought into words of Spanish, La Campaña was at his elbow, asking how much longer he would be, and in the same moment the young man disappeared on a bus.

El Líder drove off, wondering how he could have made more of this fleeting encounter with a Perfect Place antipodean, while La Campaña concentrated on the map and pointed them towards the antipodes of TUI FACTORY, MANGATAINOKA.

The village nearest Mangatainoka's antipodes was Colmenar del Arroyo. El Líder had searched it on the internet and had found out nothing about it although, using Google's translation service, he was advised of one of its customs: 'Every year in the celebrations run confinements are made of rejones of bulls and a small food of rocks in the sewer of the town.'

The explorers followed a road through the village to within three kilometres of the antipodes. Here a private road offered them a way to get even closer and La Campaña urged El Líder on past some workers' cottages to the end of the seal.

Just as the Focus pulled up, El Líder saw on the edge of the road a snake making for the long grass. It was olive green and black and he felt a shiver run up his spine.

The Tui factory was not one of his preferred Perfect Places. He had only come on the brewery by chance, and included it on the off-chance that it might somehow lead to some form of expedition sponsorship.

Now, with a snake somewhere in the grass and the sun sinking into the west somewhere beyond Portugal, El Líder was quite ready to call it a day, but La Campaña was not, and with the retreat at the Waitomo antipodes deer park still fresh in his mind, El Líder was wary of showing any further lack of commitment.

They were just 2.2 kilometres from the antipodes, it was a balmy evening, there was the prospect of a beautiful sunset, and the snake … well …

They walked along the road, which followed the crest of a hill. The hills around them were dry and stony, with trees thick in places and sparse in others. The plain below was bathed in red-gold light.

They approached a sprawling farmhouse, opened the gate, and walked across the manicured lawn, past the swimming pool, to the front door. No one appeared to be home but as they turned back to the lawn, a dog lolloped towards them, desperate to be patted, and coming up the track in the distance was an elderly couple — a big man who looked like a Spanish cattle farmer and a woman beside him who looked like a Spanish cattle farmer's wife.

El Líder was pleased to see that they were neither suspicious nor hostile and did not even seem particularly interested in who the explorers were, where they had come from, or where they wanted to go. El Líder handed over his prepared text which the man carefully read aloud in Spanish. El Líder indicated the 2.08 kilometres showing on his GPS, and waved his arm in the direction indicated by the arrow.

'Photography?' said the man.

'*Sí*,' said El Líder.

The man shrugged and from that El Líder deduced he was saying, 'If you want to go walking for two kilometres over rugged hills and through snake-infested long grass at eight o'clock at night, feel free, but it seems like an awfully stupid thing for anyone to want to do.'

'*Gracias*,' said El Líder.

He had looked up the Spanish word for snakes in the expedition phrase book and now tried out the word on the farmer.

'*Serpentine?*' he said and pointed to his sandals.

The man did not understand, so El Líder showed him the phrase book. The man said nothing but walked towards the pool and returned in a moment with a snake skin. Then, with a great deal of head-shaking and arm-waving, he explained that snakes were rarely seen. Or he might have been explaining that snakes were everywhere. El Líder was not sure.

The explorers' walk through the rough country was slow and meticulous. El Líder went in front because La Campaña refused to. Before every step, he scanned the ground to make sure that sticks and stones and shadows and holes were not in fact snakes. He made loud conversation with La Campaña until he ran out of things to say.

He moved around the side of a hill and dropped down into a valley. His head was bowed. His eyes were glued to the ground about three paces ahead.

As his foot left the ground to step over a log, there was a rustle and a snort just metres to his left. At the same instant he felt a massive thump on his backpack. His head jerked up. His heart stopped. He froze.

'El Toro!'

But it was half a dozen pigs that scampered out of the shadows, their lean hams shaking as they dashed for the hills, and the thump had been La Campaña's startled contribution to the drama.

They walked on, downhill, uphill, through valleys, around valleys. The GPS indicated that they were on the wrong side of a wire-netting fence that was higher than a deer fence by half a metre and had one strand of barbed wire along the top and another at ground level. They hunted for a weakness and found a slight dip in the ground. El Líder held up the bottom wire and La

Antipodes of Mangatainoka.

Campaña wriggled under—through the dust and the thistles. El Líder followed.

Two more fences got the same treatment—El Líder concerned each time about what the fences were keeping in besides pigs.

The sun was just a degree or two off the horizon and its soft, golden light streamed through oak trees casting long shadows on the grass and on the remains of ancient stone walls.

They came to the antipodes, and fears of snakes and bulls and rustling noises in the shadows evaporated. It was an idyllic place and El Líder set about trying to capture the antipodes of Mangatainoka on film while La Campaña searched for centrepiece possibilities.

She found a footprint in the shape she imagined a bear might leave, and although El Líder had read about bears in parts of northern Spain, this footprint was not distinct enough to make him concerned. He took the last photos as the light failed, and they headed for the Focus, keen to be out of the hills before nightfall.

El Líder recorded the details of each search for an antipodes in his expedition notebook. Already he had used up more than half his pencil. And as he flicked through what he had recorded, it reminded him of another book he had not finished reading. It was called *From North Cape to Bluff* and was written by the great walker and publisher Sir Alfred Reed who recorded all the details of his 1960 walk from Cape Reinga to Bluff when he was 85 years old.

El Líder remembered once unkindly describing the book as one of the most boring he had ever taken out of the library, because it seemed to contain nothing but the recollection of every cup of tea the old walker was offered along the way.

'About midday, as I was passing a farmhouse a little distance back from the road, a young man ran down to the gate with an invitation to lunch, and I had the pleasure of meeting Mr and Mrs Avery and their sons, who had been on the lookout for me.

'I had been told that, a few miles before arriving at Eketahuna, I might have some difficulty in crossing the Mangatainoka River, then unbridged, but that if it proved to be unfordable, I might go some distance across country to the railway bridge.

'I called at the nearest farm, at a side road a mile or so from the river, and was told by the farmer, Mr Cornelius, that as there had not been much rain lately, he thought I would be able to cross.'

And on and on it went: page after page of minute detail that only the insane or the very strange could find interesting. And, unfortunately, El Líder detected a similarity with his own notes. It seemed to be an easy mistake to spot, but one difficult to avoid, and all that could be done, he decided, was to continue on and then, perhaps, put a warning at the start or an apology at the end.

His first glimpse of the antipodes of EKATAHUNA BOWLERS IN THE SUN revealed an awkward antipodes inside a hydro-electric dam construction site guarded by workers in white helmets.

The explorers had driven to Navas del Rey—a collection of tall, bleak, stone buildings on a high, bleak plateau—and the GPS had then directed them to the construction site at the end of a narrow valley.

The obvious way to complete the final kilometre or so to the antipodes was by walking past a sign saying *Prohibito* and across the top of the dam.

The explorers were in remarkably good spirits after a night spent trying to sleep in the Focus on the side of a mountain road. The Focus had been a reliable means of transport and a regular refuge from the heat but it was an uncomfortable place to sleep. And even though El Líder had foreseen an accommodation crisis looming—as they tried and failed to find a hotel for the night—and he had downed an extra glass of *vino tinto* in a village café, he had still slept badly and woken early.

And now, with the sun barely above the horizon, they were engaged in a conversation with a Spanish foreman standing at the foot of a large, new, concrete dam.

In English, El Líder asked permission to cross.

The reply was in Spanish and appeared to be the equivalent of, 'No'.

The explorers withdrew a few kilometres and found a narrow footbridge that took them across the valley. They walked down a lane until they reached a closed metal gate from which they could see tumbledown farm buildings in the distance. There was no sign of human habitation but there was a large bull.

The explorers often made joking references to the potential danger of encountering a real-life El Toro. They had seen the famous Spanish bull represented by many huge, black-painted metal silhouettes on hillsides next to motorways, and they had picked up and put back down much of the El Toro memorabilia offered for sale in the Ronda tourist shop. They had watched El Toro routinely put to the sword on Spanish television.

They had a great deal of sympathy for the great black bull, and now here he was, directly between the expedition and its goal. Or one of its goals, El Líder reminded himself as he peered through the gate.

For once, La Campaña was hesitant about a frontal approach and they explored alternative routes until fences and difficult terrain forced them back to the gate.

El Toro had his head down, grazing. His tail flicked from side to side in what looked to El Líder like a menacing way, although he might have been swatting flies.

El Líder looked and thought, and said nothing for quite some time. He was still smarting from the defeat at the antipodes of Waitomo. Suddenly, to his own surprise, he announced that he would put El Toro to the test and go through the gate while La Campaña waited to see what happened.

La Campaña had also been thinking and almost at the same instant suggested they could return later, when the workmen had gone for the day, and cross the dam as they had originally intended.

Workmen in Spain seemed to finish at about 6 p.m. and there was light til 10 p.m. Brilliant. El Líder congratulated La Campaña on her lateral thinking and in an instant they were back in the Focus, heading away in search of breakfast.

El Líder still did not have actual Ekatahuna bowlers in the sun on film and the antipodes across the dam appeared to consist of a featureless flat area of recently bulldozed ground surrounded by low, featureless hills.

As the day wore on, his inclination to return faded and eventually they never did.

The next point would be a different matter. El Líder had been delighted with the 360-degree view at KICK-OFF POINT, MOYNIHAN PARK, SHANNON and was determined that there would be a similarly spectacular spread of photographs from its antipodes.

The GPS directed them to an area near Cebreros (pop. 3,223) directly west of Madrid in the Ávila province of Castile-Leon, the birthplace of Adolfo Suárez, Spain's first democratically elected prime minister. El Líder knew this because he had cut and pasted the Wikipedia entry into the expedition bible.

The area's high number of cloud-free days was the reason it was chosen as the site for a 35-metre deep-space antenna designed to communicate with spacecraft on long journeys to other planets, a fact courtesy of www.spacedaily.com.

But details of this sort were of only fleeting interest to the explorers who had more immediate concerns. They were parked at the entrance to a farm, contemplating another metal gate and the prospect of a three-kilometre walk up and over a substantial hill.

El Líder was developing an uncomfortable feeling about walking on private property without permission. It was not so much that he minded trespassing. It was the thought of being caught. And having to explain. And looking eccentric. Or weird. It was certainly going to be another one of those gloriously hot, dry, dusty days in the Spanish interior. And three kilometres was a distance on the borderline of what was allowed under expedition policies.

El Líder suggested to La Campaña that perhaps it would be simply good manners to try a little harder to get a little closer by driving along one of the public roads they had not yet tried.

La Campaña agreed and the Focus plunged hundreds of metres down a narrow, winding road through a series of small valleys. El Líder squinted up without relish at the steep, forested hillsides around them.

Initially they found that they were travelling away from the antipodes, but after a time, at each turn, the distance dropped by a few metres until they had just a kilometre to go and were pulling into Flores de Ávila—a picturesque mountain village of stone houses and cobbled streets.

Elderly folk with walking sticks smiled as the explorers drove slowly into the village's maze of narrow lanes, until the going was too narrow for the Focus—its wing mirrors in danger of being wiped off on the stone walls of the houses on each side.

El Líder reversed out carefully and drove to a café in the plaza for coffee, satisfied that the hard yards had been done and their goal was within easy reach. They sat outside the café on a stone

Antipodes of kick-off point, Moynihan park, Shannon.

bench in the shade, just like regular Spanish villagers, and geriatric pedestrians stopped to chat, in Spanish, not seeming to mind that they got little sense out of the explorers.

There was no sign of a shop in the village and it was only by carefully watching the comings and goings of locals that La Campaña spotted the doorway that hid the bakery, and they soon had a stick of bread to go with the bottle of pickled artichokes that had caught her eye during a *supermercado* visit.

A short drive on a gravel road brought them to a point ten metres from the antipodes of SHANNON. El Líder stepped out of the Focus and climbed onto a warm, fat rock with his camera for a fabulous view down the valley towards the village and the plain beyond. He took 24 photos.

They shared their lunch of dry bread and pickled artichokes with the inhabitants of an anthill next to the village tip, then headed back the way they had come.

El Líder had no intention of being caught short with accommodation again, so mid-afternoon they booked into a hotel in Santa Maria la Real de Nieva. La Campaña did the laundry in the bath and El Líder rigged a clothesline to allow his white shirts to drip-dry, and when they were ready, they set out to find the antipodes of STONEHENGE, NEAR CARTERTON.

It was later in the evening than seemed ideal but they had not far to walk.

At first it seemed that the antipodes would be in a field of wheat stubble with views of two church steeples, a pine forest, and a new railway line.

However, the GPS directed them under a rail bridge and deep into the pine forest, to a place which seemed to El Líder to be both uninteresting and dimly lit. Disappointed, he suggested they return in the morning.

But as they poked about in the last strands of light, the place rather grew on them. The coarse bark of the trees and the over-

Antipodes of Stonehenge, near Carterton.

sized, open cones on the dry ground created interesting shadows, and La Campaña pointed out a bleached skull on the pine needles that could be a centrepiece.

They headed back to Santa Maria la Real de Nieva's plaza and found an outside table at the only place still open. La Campaña asked for a menu but there was not one. This was a bar. Not a café. And not a restaurant.

The explorers were still confused about what the Spanish ate, and where, and when. It always seemed that the times when they were most hungry were the times when an eating place was least likely to be open. And there were no fast-food outlets.

The kindly landlady brought beer and red wine and chips and olives. It was not the dinner they had planned and El Líder was grateful that he had spent much of the previous ten years building up energy reserves for just such an expedition occasion.

Two giant storks landed on the top of a church tower above their heads and began a noisy conversation in the last of the evening light. The explorers finished a second drink, paid their bill, and strolled merrily back to their hotel where, despite the heat, and the absence of air-conditioning, they were soon sound asleep.

Breakfast was fraught. La Campaña had established the previous evening that breakfast was included in the price but, apart from *café solo* — or black coffee — there was no evidence of breakfast in the bar. She addressed a tired-looking barman, who had also been the receptionist when they arrived the previous day.

Unfamiliar with the Spanish for 'breakfast', she used a French word she knew for eating, and made eating motions with her hands. Small flies buzzed around her head and even El Líder was confused about which actions signalled breakfast and which were merely attempts to swat flies.

The barman slid across the bar a basket of sweet cakes wrapped in plastic.

Uh oh, El Líder thought, but said nothing.

'No! Toast!' demanded La Campaña in English.

There was no mistaking the dangerous look and toast soon arrived. El Líder was persuaded to put olive oil on it rather than butter, and rather liked it, although he could not imagine it becoming a habit.

Their goal was the antipodes of SAND DUNE, PARAPA-RAUMU, KAPITI COAST, and it appeared most likely it would be somewhere in the golden straw landscape that stretched from Santa Maria la Real de Nieva to the horizon in every direction.

The fields were laid out on a magnificent scale, interrupted only occasionally by brown villages with church towers, clusters of trees, fields of sunflowers, or narrow country roads.

The Paraparaumu antipodes was three kilometres from the village of Rivilla de Barajas (pop. 92) in the province of Ávila which was, according to the expedition bible, centred on the city of Ávila—famous for its ancient brown granite city walls with their 88 towers and nine gateways.

The explorers ran out of road, but were left with an easy one-kilometre walk across stubble and between large square bales of straw.

A sign indicated private property but the only person they could ask permission of was a tractor driver who had been baling straw when they arrived but was now heading away for lunch.

Soon they were alone in a huge field overlooking a castle-like building. A white horse stood in the foreground—its body bright in the sunshine but its head in the shade. El Líder decided to wait for it to lift its head or move into a better position.

While he waited, he climbed onto a bale of straw to improve the view, and photographed, as a centrepiece, the twine that held the bale together.

Antipodes of sand dune, Paraparaumu, Kapiti Coast.

The horse did not move.

Through 300 degrees the view was the same — stubble and sky. El Líder photographed it.

The horse, in the other 60 degrees, began to wander off with its head down and El Líder snapped off a couple of photographs before it completely disappeared from view.

The film ran out.

The white horse stopped, lifted its head into the sunlight, and posed.

They had lunch at Rivilla de Barajas in the shade of the village's disintegrating church in a narrow, empty street of crumbling buildings. The bread bought that morning was now hard and dry. La Campaña opened a can of anchovies to go with the mozarella and tasteless tomatoes. A thin cat full of kittens cleaned up the leftover anchovies, and the explorers set off for the antipodes of EIGHTEENTH HOLE, TITAHI BAY, WELLINGTON, a few kilometres away and once more in fields of gold. El Líder felt he had done all he could with straw and stubble at the previous point and could not bring himself to repeat the process so left without any photographs.

The same fields-of-gold problem presented itself at the antipodes of GREEN SHRUB AT TITAHI BAY, WELLINGTON, but El Líder was fond of this Perfect Place and was determined to at least give its antipodes his best shot.

The expedition bible suggested that they were near Cantalapiedra (pop. 480) which was a municipality 69 kilometres from the city of Salamanca. They could see the brown village across the plain but had no need to go there.

El Líder pointed the Focus down a white, hard-packed dirt road between stubble fields, and passed a quaint, unmistakably Spanish-style farm building on a gentle rise.

The explorers climbed out of the Focus and set off to walk the 600 metres to the antipodes.

El Líder wore his white shirt, his torn knee-length shorts and his Roman-style Merrell sandals. La Campaña was dressed in a similar way, except that at every opportunity she rolled up the bottoms of her shorts and the bottom of her top to improve her suntan.

She wore the Paddington Bear-style straw sunhat El Líder disapproved of, and the ten-dollar, pink-framed sunglasses she had bought once on a weekend expedition to Sydney.

They could see a tractor working a field in the distance and when the driver saw them, he turned his tractor towards them.

El Líder reached the antipodes in the middle of the field but did not stop, marching on to meet the tractor head on. It swung to a stop in front of them and the cab door opened.

Without breaking stride, El Líder grabbed the handrail, sprang up the metal steps and greeted the still-seated driver in his most friendly manner, explaining their purpose in a rapid stream of English. The driver replied hesitantly in Spanish.

El Líder jumped back down to the ground next to La Campaña who was peering up at the driver from beneath her hat, grabbed his camera from his backpack, and held it up for the driver to see. La Campaña smiled. Everyone smiled.

Suddenly it was clear. El Líder was, at best, an eccentric Englishman wanting to take photographs of empty spaces in the Spanish countryside. And he was a Spanish tractor driver with a great number of better things to do. He smiled weakly, closed the door, and drove off.

The pictures from the antipodes of GREEN SHRUB were bland, but saved, El Líder hoped, by the little farm building on the skyline. Stubble was the only centrepiece option.

The explorers returned to the Focus, grabbed their plastic drink bottles, and gulped down warm water that reminded El Líder of the previous night's hotel.

Antipodes of Titahi Bay, Wellington.

Of all the distinctive landmarks in New Zealand El Líder had to chose from, the Beehive was one he felt obliged to include simply because it was the place where the country's most important business was done.

Unfortunately, he had found Parliament buildings in Wellington not particularly well designed to be a Perfect Place. Not only were the 360-degree views difficult to get excited about, but there was no obvious centrepiece.

For this reason, he had chosen a place nearby — SHORELINE PLAQUE, OUTSIDE THE BEEHIVE, WELLINGTON — which not only provided a centrepiece but also a nice city view.

But the problems at Parliament were minor compared with those at its antipodes.

The Focus took the explorers to within 400 metres and at first they were heartened by the interesting photographic opportunities that presented themselves.

As they stomped through the stubble, it seemed as if they would end up with an excellent view over the village of Alaeios, with its two church towers, and soon after, it seemed as if they would end up in a field of sunflowers instead — something La Campaña had been hoping for.

But when they reached the antipodes they could barely make out the village or the sunflowers. And, worse still, they were in the centre of a patch of barren earth without any living organism for 50 metres in every direction. The thistles were dead and even the ant holes were empty.

Trying to put the best light on it, El Líder suggested that perhaps nothing would grow there because of the very fact that it was at the antipodes of the New Zealand Parliament. But it sounded rather lame, even to him.

He took the photographs. It had been a very long day and he was dispirited by their lack of luck.

Antipodes of shoreline plaque, outside the Beehive, Wellington.

Each hunt for an antipodian point began with high hopes of a stunningly interesting scene. Perhaps they would find themselves in the plaza of a beautiful Spanish village. There were so many. Perhaps they would find themselves in a bustling city full of stylishly dressed Spaniards enjoying a day's shopping and socialising. Perhaps they would find themselves in a bullring, or a lake, or a restaurant, or someone's vegetable garden or spare bedroom.

Forty million people lived in Spain but the explorers had barely come within sight of any of them. In their experience, Spain was a vast, empty country.

And even when it seemed as if they might find an antipodes where there was the sort of beautiful empty landscape that would appeal to a painter or a photographer or the maker of a television holiday programme, they had bypassed it and ended up with the mundane view next door.

All El Líder could do was to persuade himself that the narrow rules that applied to the expedition meant that it was photographing the real Spain — Spain unposed, unprepared, without make-up.

As they wandered back across the stubble to the Focus, El Líder reminded La Campaña and himself that this was an expedition, not a camera club outing, and while this barren point might not be as famous as the point at the top of Mount Everest, or as much visited as the point in Paris where the Eiffel Tower stood, it had a unique status. Nowhere else in the world but here could be the antipodes of the Beehive.

La Campaña nodded politely.

The sun was low on the horizon and El Líder's thoughts were turning to comfortable accommodation. La Campaña thought there was time left in the day for at least one more antipodes as El Líder had several from the same vicinity in Wellington.

His favourite Wellington place had been INSIDE COLO-
NIAL COTTAGE, NAIRN STREET, WELLINGTON. It was
his only indoor Perfect Place and there were happy memories of
the three little girls who had shared with the explorers their enthusiasm for the cottage.

They drove to within 200 metres of the cottage's antipodes.
From there, it appeared that the point was beyond a crop of
chickpeas and on the far side of a field of sunflowers and, as per
expedition policy, the explorers would need to go around, not over,
the crops. So they ploughed their way through the dried thistles
along the crop edges — La Campaña's sandals and increasingly
frayed socks thick with the collected seeds and sharp objects of
previous treks.

They reached a point between the sunflower crop and a four-
lane *autovía* full of fast cars and large trucks.

To cover the last five metres to the antipodes, El Líder carefully
manoeuvred through the sunflowers until, chest deep, he raised
his eyes to the horizon.

There was Alaeios not far off and, in the middle-distance,
a burly, deeply tanned Spanish farmer heading towards them
through the sunflowers.

El Líder froze and waited, expecting an angry encounter. Instead, he was greeted in the Spanish equivalent of a hail and hearty
manner by the farmer who introduced himself as Esteban from
Alaeios.

Esteban, the explorers deduced, was the owner of not only the
field of sunflowers but also the crop of chickpeas, and El Líder
was pleased now they had taken such great care of his crops. Using
sign language, El Líder explained his desire for a photograph of
the village through his sunflowers.

This was absolutely fine with Esteban who broke off a large
sunflower head and presented it to La Campaña.

El Líder took their photo as they posed together, and a long,

Antipodes Colonial Cottage, Nairn Street, Wellington.

complicated discussion began over how to get the photograph to Esteban in his village. El Líder took the opportunity to sidle off and take his photos for the antipodes of COLONIAL COTTAGE, and when he returned, the conversation was still going. He produced his pencil and notebook and Esteban wrote down his name and address.

Alaeios was a town in the province of the city of Valladolid — a city which was once the capital of the Kingdom of Spain, the place where Christopher Columbus died in 1506, and where Cervantes first published *El Ingenioso Hidalgo Don Quijote de la Mancha*, in 1605. El Líder could think of no actual reason to go there.

11

ANTIPODES OF NELSON-MARLBOROUGH

La Campaña demanded a day off from exploring and wanted to spend it in Madrid—a city El Líder knew nothing about except that it had its antipodes near Dannevirke.

Spain's quiet, country roads had been a pleasure to drive on, but as they descended into Madrid they joined a three-lane torrent of city traffic. El Líder had planned to stick to the slower-moving right-hand lane but this was where traffic joined or departed the *autovía* and was full of lane-changing hazards.

He merged briefly with the large trucks and insane men in dilapidated vans of the centre lane, before seeking refuge in the temptingly uncluttered left-hand lane. But here a Ford Focus station wagon travelling at less than 130 kilometres per hour was not welcome, and he retreated to the insane centre lane where he suspected that one small, incorrect lane change for El Líder would lead to one giant motorway disaster for Spain.

Incomprehensible road signs flicked past—*Bandas Satoras* the most frequent. La Campaña could find no translation in the expedition phrase book.

It was a very tense El Líder who eventually pulled into an underground car park and handed the Focus's keys to a cheerful attendant who pointed the way to the metro.

The first part of El Líder's day off in Madrid consisted of

leaning on cool, stone walls of expensive department stores while La Campaña shopped. He offered encouraging comments when required, but after a surprisingly short time, El Líder's carefully disguised boredom inexplicably revealed itself, and the second part of the day became a fascinating hunt for coordinates of Perfect Places around Madrid, to be used to locate the Spanish capital's antipodes in New Zealand.

To ensure that none of Madrid's finer Perfect Places escaped them, they climbed onto a double-decker tourist bus and a few minutes later, as they rounded the Plaza de Cibeles, they realised that they had found one.

In the centre of the traffic roundabout was the magnificent bronze figure of the Roman goddess of nature, Cibele, driving a chariot pulled by two lions through a fountain of water.

The backdrop was the magnificent Palacio de Comunicaciones—the Madrid Post Office—and opposite were the Banco de España and the Palacio de Linares. There were also flowers and buses and scooters and tourists.

By the time El Líder decided they should get off the double-decker, it was too late and they decided to stay on board until it completed its circuit. El Líder spent the time viewing innumerable cathedrals and historic sites, fretting over the sun being too low in the sky for good photographs, but when they returned to the Plaza de Cibeles, he was delighted to see it was no less impressive than before.

He crossed into the centre of the roundabout to take his photographs at the foot of the fountain which, according to the expedition bible, was the place where Real Madrid football fans gathered after an important win.

On this occasion, El Líder was gathered there on his own and was uncomfortably aware that he was the centrepiece in the photographs of dozens of tourists viewing the fountain from more traditional tourist vantage points. He pretended not to notice.

With the Madrid day off behind them, the explorers returned to Spain's sparsely populated countryside and turned their attention to the antipodes of INTERISLAND FERRY, COOK STRAIT.

A series of wrong turns brought them to the plaza of a tiny village where 20 or 30 locals were sitting outside a café in the sun. There was a friendly welcome from everyone present, and good, black coffee.

El Líder ordered *tapa* dishes of potatoes, sausages, and *calamares*. La Campaña — the seafood-eating vegetarian — picked at her oily *calamares* and El Líder wolfed down his greasy sausages. They had an ice-cream and left as quickly and politely as possible, Spanish *calamares* having had one chance and been found wanting.

They chose to follow out of the town a sealed but badly potholed road which soon became a dirt road with huge ruts. El Líder had a phobia about taking the same road twice, but after an uncomfortable hour in first gear he finally acceded to La Campaña's repeated suggestions and turned back.

Another route took them to a slight hill near Castronuño from which they could just make out the Duero River in the distance.

The Duero is a most important river in Spain and Portugal, not least because its marshes are a haven for nesting and hibernating water birds like mallards, shovelers, pochards and cormorants, and it waters many of the grapevines in the two countries.

The explorers walked a short distance past a manure heap and old pieces of farm machinery, and found the antipodes of COOK STRAIT FERRY surrounded by stubble fields, sunflower crops, and a gnarled pine plantation. El Líder took his photos.

The explorers spent the night in Zamora, a town *Lonely Planet* referred to as 'another strategic fortress town' and a 'subdued place' that did not figure highly on travellers' itineraries. The expedition

Antipodes of Interisland ferry, Cook Strait.

bible noted that it was in one of the best places in Western Europe to see wolves. For El Líder it would always be the place where he ordered the Spanish potato omelet and was served eggs and chips, and for La Campaña it would be the place where she lost her camera, just as there were other towns that would be remembered for her lost sunglasses and her lost phrase book. And like those items, the camera would be found only after it had been given up for lost.

They were on the way to the antipodes of WATERFRONT, PICTON, but took a wrong exit from Zamora and found themselves on a rough road made up entirely of bitumen patches. It led them to a primitive farming area with small fields of vegetables and vines surrounded by stone walls.

They passed the occasional elderly farmer surveying his farm plot from the shade of an occasional tree; they passed a hardy old woman in a straw hat hunting a flock of lean, healthy, long-legged sheep along a dusty lane, and they passed an elderly man leading a horse through the shade trees.

It was a great place for photographs but a hard place to live, as far as El Líder could tell, and the young people seemed to have recognised that and left.

They drove through a village called Escuardo, its stone-wall-lined streets designed more for animals than for cars, and emerged onto a farm track that they followed through parched fields to the end.

There they found tumbledown farm buildings, a flock of sheep enjoying the shade of one big tree, and a couple of sheep dogs tied up under another.

The owner approached in a little white van and the explorers, with 800 metres to go, set about miming their intentions — La Campaña throwing in Spanish words at random, and occasional French and Italian. It went badly. El Líder was not sure if there was a lack of understanding or a lack of approval and, in exasperation, drew '800 m' in the dirt, and an arrow to make sure their intentions were clear.

But the seemingly friendly elderly farmer and his suspicious side-kick would not let them go on. El Líder deduced that they were concerned about a new crop in the direction the explorers wanted to procced. So that was Picton.

The explorers gave up without a fight—El Líder reminding himself that he had chosen the Perfect Place in Picton in haste and, photographically, it did not match his other Perfect Places so was not really worth fighting over. And besides, not getting into fights with elderly sheep farmers would probably soon become another expedition policy anyway.

El Líder was determined there would be no similar failure at their next point, the antipodes of the CENTRE OF NEW ZEALAND, NELSON. This would be their one-and-only foray into Portugal—or more precisely, Portugal's north-eastern district of Bragança.

As they drove unchecked across the border, they left behind the primitive Spanish villages of stone and sagging tile roofs and rough, patched roads, and noticed a greater level of prosperity.

The road led to one of the region's more major towns, Moga-douro (pop. 10,792), but before they got there they were directed by the GPS to turn off onto a narrow road to a small, lonely church deep in a valley known as the Val de Porco.

Beyond the church, three kilometres from the antipodes, the road became too rough for the Focus and El Líder was forced to turn back.

Another side-road led them through a small collection of buildings known as Vilar de Porco and onto a farm track that crossed rolling hills of dry, red, rocky soil and passed through crops of wheat and olives.

They stopped on a spur 877 metres from the antipodes. El

Líder loaded up his camera with film and his backpack with water and they set off down a pleasant walking track to the narrow, hidden valley floor where more intensive farming was evident on the better, irrigated soil.

The climb up the other side began well enough. They pushed through a thicket of old and new oak trees, upwards through roughly cultivated land, and past cork trees into an area where pines had been recently harvested.

Here, the ground was covered by a deep layer of dry, jagged pine branches which made walking slow and difficult. Worse was to come.

They were soon in an area where the leg-ripping pine was overgrown with tall, woody scrub which El Líder had to force his way through, La Campaña following closely enough behind to be swatted by springy branches.

They were counting progress by the metre. Between two drink stops they progressed only 16 metres. Small tracks that promised easy passage faded to nothing, leaving the explorers facing a wall of scrub.

Blackberry grabbed at them and sometimes trapped them. They were bleeding from a thousand scratches.

Sweat and sunscreen were running off El Líder's forehead into his eyes so, at times, he could not see where to put his feet. He thought about the moment when they would be physically unable to go forward, but could not imagine what would happen then. Going back would be just as difficult as continuing on, and he was suddenly aware that no one in the entire world knew where they were — or even that they were in Portugal.

Metre by metre they pushed their way upwards. The GPS's direction arrow had become inaccurate because it needed them to be moving along at a faster speed than they were capable of, and El Líder hoped they were still heading in the right direction.

Although La Campaña was in remarkably good spirits

Antipodes of centre of New Zealand, Nelson.

considering the toll on her legs from the thorns and dried branches, El Líder decided, just for the moment, that he would not mention the GPS problem.

Eventually, with just 20 metres to go, he could see a clearing but no easy way of getting there. He clenched his teeth and launched himself at the wall of dry scrub, and suddenly he had broken free.

They were at the antipodes of Nelson but, better still, they were out of the scrub and on an outcrop of large, round, friendly rocks. They drank the water from the backpack. El Líder was content to stay awhile and soak up the achievement but La Campaña urged him to hurry up and get the photographs so they could leave. She stood swatting flies until he had finished, then they plunged off down the hill. The scrub was easier to tackle from above and, no longer dictated to by the GPS, they avoided adding to their assortment of scratches.

At the bottom of the valley again, they found a cool stream to wash off the blood.

El Líder was already dreaming of a cool, air-conditioned hotel room but, once in the Focus, La Campaña was demanding the coordinates for the next antipodes and was talking about tent sites they had passed earlier in the day.

The explorers set their sights on the antipodes of HIGHFIELD ESTATE WINERY, BLENHEIM, which the expedition bible suggested they would find near São João das Arribas.

El Líder stopped to ask a woman on a donkey for directions and it was not long before they were in the narrow cobbled streets of the ancient, tumbledown village.

The road ended at the deep chasm of the Rio Duero, and the GPS indicated that Highfield was still five kilometres away and on the far side of the river. They would need to find a bridge but as it was already late they turned back for the campsite.

El Líder thought that after the tent was erected, a visit to a restaurant would naturally follow, but La Campaña pointed out that he had already had toast for breakfast and a sandwich for lunch, and after two small, cold glasses of Super Bock beer and a packet of crisps at the camp café, he no longer cared.

While La Campaña did the laundry, he sat in the darkness, enjoying the cool, insect-free night and the cheerful chatter of the people around him who were enjoying good beer, good coffee and good company. He had no idea if they were speaking Spanish or Portuguese.

At dawn he was woken by an owl hooting in a tree above the tent. Earlier in the morning he had been woken by another type of bird with an unusually raucous and repetitive cry. A pack of yelping puppies had woken him at one point, and a village full of roosters at another. The cold had woken him once and La Campaña had woken him innumerable times, accusing him of snoring. It seemed as though he had barely slept.

The Portuguese camping ground showers were every bit as good as those in a New Zealand camping ground, though more water came out of the shower-head than the drain could cope with immediately, and there was nowhere to hang a towel though that did not bother El Líder who had forgotten to pack one.

As he left the shower, the sun was shining through the pines, a slight mist obscured the horizon, and there was a pleasant South Island-style summer's morning chill in the air.

The explorers' morale was somewhere between excellent and better than El Líder had hoped. Each day brought a new adventure—a surprise destination to be found in no travel guide—and the anticipation reminded El Líder of the excitement of unwrapping presents at Christmastime. The fact that, so far, they'd unwrapped nothing but handkerchiefs, socks and after-shave did not dampen his enthusiasm because there was always the chance the next antipodes would be a glorious scene to match the Perfect Places he had hand-picked in New Zealand.

Once or twice he had been tempted to cheat, after arriving at an antipodes, and to move a step or two closer to a more interesting vantage point. But, in the end, all the North Island's antipodes had been photographed as they were. A true record. And that was the difference — the difference between explorers' photographs and tourist photographs.

El Líder the tourist was not immune from avoiding reality by avoiding the ugly in his photos. He had never, for instance, hesitated to leave out electricity substations, scungy ponds, scruffy vegetation, squalid industrial areas and unkempt suburbs. And while he could quite easily take a photograph of a beautiful, or expensive, or unusual car, he could never bring himself to take photographs of cars en mass.

The difference was highlighted at lunch on the way to the antipodes of Highfield. The explorers stopped by a small field of grapevines enclosed by a rock wall. A lone pine tree threw a patch of shadow onto the sun-scorched ground and the explorers made their way to it. But as they arrived with their plastic bags of food, they found that ants had claimed the shade.

So, rather than disturb them, the explorers stood in the sun next to the rock wall as they ate with their bread cocktail onions, olives, and gherkins on toothpicks, from a jar La Campaña had chosen from a *supermercardo*.

They had forgotten to pack a knife but luckily El Líder's West-pac Gold Card was an excellent tool for cutting tomatoes and spreading margarine.

They gazed about them as they chewed. It was a beautiful part of the countryside. As well as the rock walls and vines, there were golden hills in the distance and scattered villages with tile roofs.

But right through the scene ran a power line on the ugliest metal poles El Líder had ever seen. And across the road there was a small rubbish tip.

La Campaña set about taking a tourist photograph. By standing in the right place, she was able to frame out the power lines and the tip — and the ants were hidden by a rock wall—so that when they left, they had a photograph featuring the beauty of the Spanish (or was it Portuguese?) countryside without its blemishes. A perfect tourist photograph.

El Líder's enthusiasm for finding the next point was keen, but La Campaña had embraced the idea with a drive and determination that left him feeling almost half-hearted. No sooner had one point been photographed than La Campaña was demanding to be off to the next. With maps on her lap and GPS at hand, she steered the expedition through road systems that had yet to be drawn on their elderly map of Europe.

The antipodes of Highfield Estate was not high on El Líder's agenda but La Campaña steered them in that direction anyway. There were more narrow roads between rock walls that led to more narrow village streets, then more narrow farm roads and eventually their path became just a faint imprint on grass where a tractor had once been driven.

They were about three kilometres inside the Portuguese border, a kilometre from the village of Bemposta, and 900 metres from the Highfield antipodes.

El Líder slung his bag on his back and they set out again. To the left through an old gateway in a stone wall was a field of long grass and shady trees; to the right some cultivated ground where grapevines sprang up randomly from the red soil.

In the distance El Líder could see a herd of cattle. He could tell one was a bull though it was uncharacteristically brown.

Like a magnet, El Toro drew the GPS towards him until the inevitable moment when the expedition needed to decide if it should squeeze through strands of rusty barbed wire and enter the bull's domain.

'Don't worry. He'll be fine. He's only interested in the cows,' La Campaña, the experienced cowgirl, recited every so often.

El Líder, though, had no interest in bravery merely for show, and took an indirect route towards Highfield that kept the fence between them and the bull.

He had seen a vehicle parked in the neighbouring field, and made his way towards it. A farmer and his worker were amongst the cattle, gently separating out some cows—quietly and expertly guiding them without dogs or noise.

In a good-natured, businesslike way, the farmer indicated that the explorers were welcome to enter the paddock with the cattle so long as they did not leave the gate open. El Líder tried to make a joke about El Toro but the two men did not seem to understand and climbed into their farm truck and drove off.

The cattle had moved to the other end of the paddock, and El Toro seemed to be distracted by one particular cow for the moment, so the explorers slipped into the paddock and walked to the antipodes.

They stopped and gazed at the featureless landscape around them. It could be anywhere in the entire world of cattle farming.

El Líder took some photographs and began studying the nearer surroundings. There were butterflies whose wings were a rich burnt-orange when they were flying but a dreary light brown when they landed and folded them up. El Líder could not manage to capture one in all its glory on film so La Campaña offered to kill one and spread it out for El Líder to photograph. He declined.

He found a new variety of thistle with quite an attractive blue flower, then he spotted some red insects on the head of another thistle variety—providing a pleasant contrast—but they refused

Antipodes of Highfield Estate, Blenheim.

to pose in the right place for a photograph. A yellow insect on a daisy did oblige and La Campaña contributed a huge grasshopper.

El Toro came closer, although not in a threatening way, and El Líder, happy with his photographs, headed for the fence at a relaxed but determined pace.

La Campaña had been haunted by flies during many of their Spanish walks but on this occasion, as they meandered through small fields of grapes and larger fields of newly mown hay, separated by rustic stone walls, she was accompanied by clouds of brightly coloured butterflies, and this time there were no flailing arms and loud complaints. The walk back to the Focus took about an hour but El Líder would have been happy to do it twice over.

LAKE GRASSMERE HUT UNDER GREY SKIES was one of the Perfect Points that El Líder remembered best, and now they were within 200 metres of its antipodes south of the town of Toro and just beyond Valdefinjas (pop. 96) — a tiny, medieval-looking stone village famous, according to the internet, for its home-made wine.

They were stopped at the end of a farm road within sight of a large reservoir, their way barred by an outcrop of scrub which El Líder declared he was not prepared to enter under any circumstances.

They began working their way around the outside, and descended into a dried-up arm of the reservoir — the last remnants of dampness promoting a vivid green-yellow carpet over the valley floor and raising El Líder's hopes of a visually interesting antipodes.

Wherever they walked, they stepped on herbs which threw up their perfume, and El Líder swore he could smell curry.

Hedged in by the scrub, the explorers were gaining on the

Antipodes of Lake Grassmere hut.

antipodes by only one metre in every 20 metres they walked and, eventually, the GPS arrow was pointing at more than 90 degrees, leaving them with no choice but to stop and contemplate the steep face covered in scrub.

There were only 30 metres to go and El Líder told La Campaña to wait and she did not object as El Líder began climbing. His chances of capturing the colourful valley receded as he moved further and further into the dense scrub. He was tempted to turn back and claim that the going was too hard but each time he was tempted, another small clear space opened up, so at no point could he claim that his way was totally blocked.

Eventually, he reached a gnarled shade tree—which just happened to be the antipodes of Grassmere—and he set about taking photographs. The beautiful greens of the valley floor were mostly obscured.

The bark of the tree harboured hundreds of fat flies which took to the air as soon as El Líder went near it, and a mosquito whizzed around his ear. It took only a very short time to gather his photographs.

It was almost midnight when the hot and grimy explorers, in sandals and shorts, found a hotel. It had marble stairways, a plush lounge, stacks of new antiques, and a glass-fronted lift. The receptionist was polite.

La Campaña borrowed a corkscrew from the bar and they opened the cheap bottle of red wine, polished off almost half of it, and collapsed for the night, as drunk as lords.

12

ANTIPODES OF CANTERBURY

Only the Canterbury antipodes were left to find. El Líder had more Perfect Points than he knew what to do with, so decided to narrow down his Canterbury eight to three. He was disappointed to lose SOFT ROCK AT CASTLE HILL, CANTERBURY, and HARD ROCK AT RAKAIA GORGE, and a little guilty to be skipping Hamner — the source of the 'Do not go where the path may lead …' expedition motto, courtesy of Waldo Emerson — but they were running out of time. The Focus had to go back to the rental car company.

Searching for the antipodes of RAILWAY STATION, SHEFFIELD, CANTERBURY, the expedition travelled through forested hills, crossed clear, clean rivers, and passed through rustic villages. In places, huge new motorways carved through the landscape, and every hilltop had a row of modern, white, wind turbines waiting for a breeze.

They followed a narrow, sealed road that wound its way into sparsely populated valleys full of trees. Every time it seemed that the road was about to end at a collection of stone farm buildings, a sliver of sealed road continued on.

Six kilometres from the antipodes, El Líder was pessimistic. Surely they would not be able to penetrate the steep valleys much further by road, and he certainly had no desire to walk that distance.

Much of the forest was radiata pine and eucalyptus, and in between the rows were El Líder's old enemies—gorse and blackberry.

They pushed on, taking the next right or the next left at the whim of the GPS, and were within a kilometre and a half of the antipodes when they mistakenly took a private farm road.

The farmer's mother was sunbathing at the back door, and while she dressed rapidly, El Líder did a three-point turn in her backyard.

They stopped, finally, in a deserted part of the forest.

They were near Feira do Monte, Cospeito, east of Vilalba and north of Lugo. They were also next to a footpath that led them through the shade of mature pines into a picturesque hay paddock.

From there, the path became overgrown with New Zealand-style ferns, then faded out completely on reaching an Australian-style stand of young eucalypts.

La Campaña pushed gorse and blackberry aside with a stick until the blackberry became too much. As well, the hill was becoming very steep. Far beneath their feet they could make out a lake through the trees. The air was dense and humid.

El Líder ate ripe blackberries for a few minutes, then they retraced their steps and found an easier way down through some native trees to the lake edge.

The GPS was pointing to the antipodes about 100 metres away, across a narrow neck of water. El Líder was tempted to take the photograph from where they were but the light was wrong.

They edged slowly around the steep, slippery lake shore, crawling through scrub and trees until they found the end of the arm, a grotto-like area of dark, deep-green water and overhanging native forest.

El Líder fancied the antipodes would be on the small knoll of wildflowers, surrounded on three sides by water and caught in a shaft of sunlight. He couldn't wait.

They crossed a stream that tumbled into the lake—the GPS pointing fair and square at the flowery knoll.

As they advanced, El Líder glanced anxiously at the GPS. The number of metres was dropping, but very slowly. It soon became obvious that they would not be stopping where El Líder had hoped and they began climbing back into the forest.

El Líder could not let go of the antipodes of wildflowers with its view over the lake. The GPS had to be wrong.

He ran ahead, up the hill, and emerged at the top—his way blocked by a barbed wire fence interwoven with blackberry. Peering upwards, he could see a clearing that contained eucalypts in bright sunshine. It could be Australia or New Zealand.

He turned back down the hill in disgust and encountered La Campaña still on the way up. He told her he was heading for the wildflowers.

She objected. What about the rule? 'We're not here to take pretty pictures,' she told him.

They climbed back to the eucalypts and studied the scene more closely. For better or worse, this was the antipodes of RAILWAY STATION, SHEFFIELD, CANTERBURY.

A Red Admiral butterfly took a shine to La Campaña and attached itself to her back, and an array of different-coloured butterflies and hopping insects kept the explorers amused for ages.

They drank the cold water they had brought along and headed back to the Focus with the help of the GPS, finding an easier way than before and, after the intensity of the hunt for the antipodes, spent more time enjoying the surroundings.

Their arrival at the north coast of Spain signaled that the expedition was nearly over. They were in Foz which the expedition bible revealed to be a fishing port 140 kilometres from the Galician capital of A Coruña, with a population of 10,000 people, and regarded as idyllic on the tourist website where it was mentioned.

El Líder was tired and grumpy. The expedition had failed to produce that magical moment of triumph — the instance when the first foot was placed on the moon, the first view of Victoria Falls was had, or the final step was taken to the top of Everest.

'To our immense satisfaction, we realized we had reached the top of the world!

'It was 11.30 a.m. on 29th May 1953. In typical Anglo-Saxon fashion, I stretched out my arm for a handshake, but this was not enough for Tenzing who threw his arms around my shoulders in a mighty hug and I hugged him back in return.'

And here they were in Foz — a town well-used to the point of being shabby. El Líder decided, sweepingly and unkindly, that it lacked charm. He was, therefore, cynically amused to find that the bathroom of their hotel — O Northe — was equipped with sachets of shampoo and bath gel called A Touch of Charm. Obviously he was wrong about Foz.

It was almost midnight before they began thinking of dinner. They walked to the beach, found a bar, and sat outside in the balmy darkness drinking the local brew which El Líder found was not San Miguel but never mind.

They found a restaurant selling meat and El Líder ordered whatever the waiter suggested which turned out to be a piece of pork fat on bone. But never mind.

The wine was cheap and easy to drink.

El Líder had decided it would be paranoid of him to take the GPS into town in order to find their way back to the hotel without getting lost, so after paddling along the beach and admiring the lights of Foz, they spent a very long time walking the dark backstreets to their small, damp, malodorous hotel room.

O Northe offered bedside ashtrays—a sign La Campaña would have picked up on if she had inspected the room before agreeing to take it. But another late-night finish to a long, weary day had left the expedition vulnerable.

Increasingly, the explorers had found pretty much anything acceptable at night and only began to notice their mistakes in the morning. O Northe was one such mistake.

By nine o'clock La Campaña was ready for breakfast, but the man behind the bar downstairs was not, and she sat and waited pointedly—perusing the local newspaper for any words of English.

After coffee and croissants, the explorers left for the beach where El Líder sat in the Focus in the car park and enjoyed, from a distance, the calm waters of the Bay of Biscay with its clean white beaches, while La Campaña went for a walk. She found a used condom in the car park and a bad smell at the beach.

Their next destination was the antipodes of THE SQUARE, CHRISTCHURCH. As they drove through the northern country-side in the morning light, El Líder enjoyed the children's story-book views of meadows with cows, fields of corn, tidy woodlands, smooth, sealed roads, and neat three-storey farmhouses. They passed an elderly couple turning hay with large wooden forks. One internet site had described the Galicia countryside as 'romantic' and El Líder, his good mood restored by warm country scenes, could not deny it.

Two point two kilometres from the antipodes of The Square, they stopped. There was every chance that they could drive to a closer point by exploring other roads, but the weather was good and the walking track leading off into a forest of eucalypts looked inviting.

They climbed steadily for a kilometre and El Líder thought, with just 1.2 kilometres of downhill ahead of them, that the worst was over.

The track was now paved with dried gorse and the sandal-clad explorers picked their way carefully down a slope which was moderate to begin with and then much steeper.

La Campaña could cope with the gorse, with the heat and the steep slope. But she would have no part of the flies. She could not abide a fly within 20 metres of her, and while she was permanently engaged in fending off gorse bushes with a stick in one hand, the other hand was continuously flying around her head.

The 'f' word was one she reserved almost exclusively for flies. Whether they were big fat dozey ones, cheerful flittering ones, insane dive bombers or friendly clingers, to La Campaña they were all 'f…ing flies'. And as the explorers made their way down the track, the 'f' flies were the main topic of conversation.

Eventually they had no choice but to part company with the track and plunge off into the undergrowth.

El Líder had said that nothing would induce him to do this again, but now they were only 480 metres from the antipodes of Christchurch.

They carved their way through patches of cool, willowy ferns, found plain sailing beneath pine trees, pranced through young eucalypts and soft green gorse bushes, and finally emerged onto a forestry road. Fifty metres later they were there.

They could no longer make out the imposing peak of Pico da Frouxeira and they had no idea where they were — their view in every direction blocked by trees.

As he climbed a rock to take photographs, El Líder slipped, making a loud noise which disturbed a wild deer. It ran off into the forest with an appalling bark. El Líder missed his chance to photograph it in the distance and had to content himself with butterflies and flowers.

La Campaña was hoping they could take a more friendly route back to the Focus, and they decided to follow a reasonably well-formed track to the skyline. It grew steeper the nearer the summit

Antipodes of the Square, Christchurch.

they got, and above them were great round boulders, each bigger than a house, and to the right and left slopes covered in thick forest and gorse.

Fifty metres from the top they could go no further. Their way was blocked by boulders too high and smooth to climb and gorse too vicious to push through.

El Líder was disappointed. La Campaña was just plain angry as they gingerly retraced their route down the perilously slippery track. They tried a side track but once again ran into gorse.

Luckily, El Líder had taken some GPS positions along the way and knew that although they appeared to be quite lost, he could find a point that would get them back onto their original route from the Focus.

When they found the track paved with gorse, which had seemed such an ordeal earlier, it felt like a familiar friend and they barely noticed the pain.

It had taken them four hours to complete the four-kilometre round trip.

Back at the Focus, El Líder lay down on a picturesque patch of long grass beneath a shady tree and took a long drink of water.

He was content to rest there a while, but La Campaña was instantly in the car, and had it started so that the air-conditioning would work. With the noise and the diesel fumes drifting in El Líder's direction, the moment was lost and he climbed wearily into the Focus and drove off in search of their last antipodean point, FISHING OFF THE PIER, NEW BRIGHTON.

They found it not far from the one for Christchurch Square—not surprisingly—but the terrain was so similar that El Líder decided not to waste film on it.

And that was pretty much it. They could call the expedition over, right there, amongst the gorse on the opposite side of the planet to THE SQUARE, CHRISTCHURCH.

La Campaña had had enough and so had El Líder. Although …

There was just one more place he wanted to go — the place El Líder had calculated was the most northerly place in Spain with a New Zealand antipodes. It would provide them with a set of coordinates to find south of Christchurch.

So they set out for the Cape of Ortegal and after passing through a confusing little village, they were there — at the lighthouse.

People took photographs of each other and looked down on the churning sea and towards the horizon, little realising that they were opposite a cow paddock in mid-Canterbury, perhaps, or halfway up a scree slide in the Southern Alps, or somewhere in the bush.

El Líder was struggling to know how to end the expedition. Here they were, standing on the other side of the world, with New Zealand buzzing along upside down beneath their feet — or at this time of day more likely tucked up in bed. But it did not seem that special. It was too hard to grasp the big picture. As usual, there were too many little pictures: Had he locked the car? Was it parked where it would not get bumped? Did he want his photo taken in front of the lighthouse?

And after they left the lighthouse, it was all about navigating narrow streets, finding the right money for the motorway toll-operator, and locating a hotel.

Waldo Emerson would no doubt have had something fitting to say at the end of an expedition like this, but El Líder himself could not really think of anything.

POSTSCRIPT

El Líder was limping with one strained ankle and one grazed ankle. It was a difficult to decide how to limp for best effect.

There were a great many limpers where they were waiting to catch their plane for England. The explorers were in Santiago de Compostela, not far from the antipodes of THE SQUARE, where thousands of footsore Catholics, having walked the pilgrim trail, were basking in their own moment of glory.

With their walking sticks, odd hats, scallop shells, boots, and backpacks, they were lolling about in the streets and plazas around the cathedral, revelling in their achievements.

El Líder was also revelling a little, but was dressed less conspicuously in cheap canvas shoes and track pants. The explorers walked to a park and found a comfortable bench in the shade, overlooking the cathedral.

El Líder sat quietly and gazed about him — his notebook on his lap. La Campaña struggled to write a postcard in Spanish to someone from their language class.

Above the roar of traffic, he could hear gentle guitar music wafting from the nearby market. A man next to him shouted in bad English into his cellphone something about coffee. A young couple sitting on the grass studied a map of the city. A sparrow rested on a rock. A vagrant slept in the shade next to his plastic bags.

For each, for the moment, this was a Perfect Place, and El Líder suspected that none of them gave a damn where its antipodes was.

La Campaña swore about the sentence she was trying to write.

El Líder brought out the Garmin Etrex, his new best friend, and asked which way they needed to go to regain the Focus.

The expedition was over.

He put his notebook away and got up to go.

'Don't stop now. Keep writing. I haven't finished the postcard yet.' These instructions from La Campaña.

El Líder sat down and got his notebook out again. He wondered if an expedition could truly be an expedition unless it was shared with the world.

The final chapter, he decided, would be devoted to the details of how the story of the Journey to the Ends of the Earth came to be published in a book.

El Líder looked at the stub of his pencil. No, bugger it, he decided. This was the end.

BIBLIOGRAPHY

Every effort was made to contact copyright holders
for material quoted in this book.

The Barbary Slaves, Stephen Clissold, Totowa NJ, 1977.

El Ingenioso Hidalgo Don Quijote de la Mancha, Miguel de Cervantes Saavedra,
published by Francisco de Robles, 1605.

From North Cape to Bluff: On Foot at Eighty-five, A.H. Reed, A.H. & A.W.
REED, Wellington, 1961.

Insight Guide Morocco, edited by Dorothy Stannard, Apa Publications,
London, England, 2006.

Insight Guide Southern Spain, APA Publications GmbH & Co. Singapore
branch, Fourth Edition 2006.

Journeys of the Great Explorers, Rosemary Burton, Richard Cavendish, and
Bernard Stonehouse, Automobile Association, Hampshire, 1992.

Livingstone's African Journal 1853–1856, edited with introduction by
I. Schapera, Vol I, Chatto and Windus Ltd, London, 1963.

Northern Spain, Andy Syminton, Footprint Travel Guide Series, Bath, UK,
2005.

Tapas, the Little Dishes of Spain, Penelope Casas, Pavilion Books, London, UK,
1985.

The Tin Can Band and Other Poems, Margaret Mahy, Puffin Books, Penguin,
London, England, 1989.

View From The Summit, Sir Edmund Hillary, Doubleday/Random House New
Zealand, Auckland, New Zealand, 1999.

Websites
The *Guardian* online, Seabed gold 'clue to white slavers', http://www.guardian.
co.uk
http://i-cias.com/morocco/lixus.htm

http://www.geocities.com/laracheweb/lixus.htm
http://translate.google.com/translate
http://www.answers.com/topic/antipodal-point
www.peakbagger.com
http://ccat.sas.upenn.edu/jod/twayne/aug1.html
http://www.world66.com/africa/morocco/larache
http://i-cias.com/morocco/larache.htm
http://www.virtualtourist.com/travel/Africa/Morocco/Province_de_Larache/
 Larache-2111470/Local_Customs-Larache-BR-1.html#1
http://www.peakware.com/areas.html?a=369
http://communities.co.nz/kerikeri/History.cfm
http://www.perseus.tufts.edu/Herakles/labors.html
http://www.expat.or.id/info/mozaic.html
http://www.transcendentalists.com/emerson_quotes.htm
http://www.geocities.com/rwe1844/bio/porte_bio.htm
http://www.domsalt.co.nz/profile.html
http://www.colonialcottagemuseum.co.nz/history.html
http://www.eztrip.com/dg_viewLocation_locationId-36758.html
http://berclo.net/page99/99en-morocco.html
http://www.i-cias.com/morocco/larache.htm
http://www.world66.com/africa/morocco/larache
http://www.xenophilia.com/zb0008h.htm
hypertextbook.com/facts/1999/RicardoMartinez.shtml
http://pubs.usgs.gov/gip/interior/
http://www.physlink.com/education/askexperts/ae52.cfm
http://en.wikipedia.org/wiki/The_Answer_to_Life,_the_Universe,_and_
 Everything
http://www.tiscali.co.uk/reference/encyclopaedia/hutchinson/m0001781.html
http://www.searchiberia.com/articles/publish/article_23.shtml
http://www.essentialmagazine.com
http://www.andalucia.com/ronda/home.htm
http://www.turismoderonda.es/geografiahistoria/eng/historia.htm
http://www.andalucia.com/history/acinipo.htm
http://www.turismoderonda.es/excursiones/eng/elgastor.htm
http://www.andalucia.com/province/malaga/alameda/tempranillo.htm
http://genealogy.about.com/b/a/255819.htm
http://www.unmaskingcolumbus.com/unmasking_columbus/
 ChristopherColumbus_ch01.htm
http://www.imageone.com/goya/

http://www.guiacampsa.com/bienvenidoalinfinito/gcampsa/ocioviajes/
rutasturismo/rutas4.asp

http://en.wikipedia.org/wiki/Battle_of_Bail%C3%A9n

http://en.wikipedia.org/wiki/La_Mancha

http://www.cheesefromspain.com/CFS/1505Manchego_I.htm

http://en.wikipedia.org/wiki/Cebreros

http://www.spacedaily.com/news/esa-general-05s.html

http://en.wikipedia.org/wiki/Cantalapiedra

http://en.wikipedia.org/wiki/Valladolid

http://www.aviewoncities.com/madrid/plazadecibeles.htm

http://columbia.thefreedictionary.com/Duero+River

http://www.answers.com/topic/mogadouro

http://it.wikipedia.org/wiki/Venialbo

http://www.pueblos-espana.org/castilla

http://en.orangetravel.eu/en/HolidayHomes/FozRiasAltas/0,2327,133999,00.
html

http://www.travelistic.com/blog_post/show/275

http://www.californiamall.com/holidaytraditions/traditions-spain.htm

http://eventsuk.britishairways.com/sisp/index.htm?fx=event&event_id=26955

http://en.wikipedia.org/wiki/Charles_II_of_England

http://en.wikipedia.org/wiki/Trabancos_River

http://www.red2000.com/spain/region/r-cleon.html

http://www.spanish-living.com/regional/indexR_Castilla_Leon.htm

http://en.wikipedia.org/wiki/Andalusia

http://www.andalucia.com/bullfight/home.htm

http://www.red2000.com/spain/region/r-galic.html

http://www.idealspain.com/Pages/Food/castillayleonwine.htm

http://www.zefrank.com/sandwich/tool.html